Three Children's Plays

Three Children's Plays

The Poet and the Rent
The Frog Prince
The Revenge of the Space Pandas or
Binky Rudich and the Two-Speed Clock

by David Mamet

Grove Press, Inc./New York

First Grove Press Edition 1986
First Printing 1986
ISBN: 0-394-55302-0
Library of Congress Catalog Card Number: 86-45245

First Evergreen Edition 1986
First Printing 1986
ISBN: 0-394-62167-0
Library of Congress Catalog Card Number: 86-45245

Designed by David Miller.

Printed in the United States of America

GROVE PRESS, INC., 920 Broadway, New York, N.Y. 10010

5 4 3 2 1

This collection is dedicated to W. H. Macy

CONTENTS

The Poet and the Rent

*A Play for Kids
from Seven to 8:15*

CHARACTERS

Aunt Georgie, *a camp counselor*
Sergeant Albert Pressman, *a mountie*
Kodiak Prince, *a wonderdog*
The Poet, *a poet*
The Landlord, *a landlord*
The Girlfriend, *a young woman*
Spuds O'Malley, *a cop who keeps his eyes peeled*
The Factory Owner, *a capitalist*
The Wacko Woman, *an advertising copywriter*
Gene, *a thief*
Boots, *a thief*
Various other people

The Poet and the Rent is dedicated to W. H. Macy, in the hopes that he and I may continue to be aware of what the other is thinking; and, Ladies and Gentlemen, to Patricia Cox.

This play takes place in a theater. All of the characters, at various times, address the audience directly, and most men and women in their time play many parts.

Aunt Georgie *(blows whistle):* Hello and welcome, Boys and Girls. I'm Aunt Georgie and you're Children, and today we're going to bring you that perennial classic, "The Poet and the Rent."

But first I'd like to introduce to you your favorite storyteller, Sergeant Albert Pressman of the Yukon, and his wonderful Wonderdog, Kodiak Prince, the Wonderdog . . .

Pressman: Hello, Boys and Girls, I'm . . .

Aunt Georgie: . . . those two Ace Crime Preventers of the Frozen North, we're glad to have them here!

Pressman: We're glad to be here. *(Pause.)* Hello, Boys and Girls, I'm Sergeant Pressman of the Yukon, and this is Kodiak . . .

Aunt Georgie: . . . Kodiak Prince. A wonderful dog, and a great Human Being. As you know, kids . . . **(Prince** *hits* **Aunt Georgie** *in the face with a pie. Pause.)* Alright. Alright. But there's nothing on God's Green Earth that's going to keep me from making sure that these children have a wonderful experience in the Theater this afternoon. *(Pause. Exits.)*

Pressman: Hello, Boys and Girls. I'm Sergeant Albert Pressman of the Yukon, and this, of course, is Prince, The Wonderdog.

Prince: Bow Wow.

Pressman: And now Wacko presents, "The Poet and the Rent." **(Prince** *hands* **Pressman** *the* Old Storybook. **Press-**

man *reads.)* "Once Upon a Time, in a Theater very much like this one, a young poet sat in his apartment . . . and he said: *(Read simultaneously with* **Poet's** *first line.)*

(In the **Poet's** *apartment.)*

Poet: I love the World. I'm very fond of it. I love the little rain that clears the air of noxious vapors, and the dear cracked sidewalk that will lead me where I want to go.

I love the little children in their schools, and Older People — but still useful to society — sitting in the Park and talking about Ducks. I have everything a young man could want. *(Pause.)* Except one thing.

Offstage Voice: What's that?

Landlord: I'll tell you what that is! It's the rent. He doesn't have the Rent! *(Knocks on* **Poet's** *door.)*

Poet: Who's there?

Landlord: The Landlord.

Poet *(to audience):* The Landlord! *(Pause.)*

I love the Landlord, he's the one who turns on all the
  heat.
He polishes the mailbox and keeps the hallways neat.
He always sweeps the sidewalk, and he takes the gar-
  bage out.
But when he . . .

Landlord *(busts into the apartment):* Don't give me that drivel. Give me the rent. The rent is two weeks overdue.

Poet: But I can explain why.

Landlord: Alright. Why? *(To audience:)* This better be good.

Poet: I don't have it.

Landlord: Well, you better have it by noon tomorrow, or out in the street you go. *(Exits.)*

Poet: Yeah!!!?

Landlord *(re-enters):* Yeah! *(Exits.)*

Poet *(sighs):* Looks like that is that. *(Picks up telephone and dials.)*

Operator: Information . . .

Poet: Hello, Information. How do I go about getting sixty dollars by tomorrow noon?

Operator: *How* much do you need, sir?

Poet: Sixty dollars. S as in Sam. I as in In. X as in Wacko. T as in . . .

Operator: Yes sir. Just one moment. I will connect you with my supervisor.

Supervisor: Supervisor, Miss Priss. Sixty dollars is a lot of Bananas to come up with overnight. That is all the information I am allowed to give out. *(Hangs up.)*

Poet: Thanks for nothing. *(Hangs up. To audience:)* Biggest corporation in the country, huh! *(Sighs.)* I have an idea. I've got it! I will write my poems for money! I shall sell the fruit of my labor! *(To cast:)* Okay, everybody! Out to the Park!

(The cast comes out and strikes 'the apartment' set and sets up "the park" set. The Park. The **Poet** *is sitting on a bench writing in his book.)*

Tree . . . bumblebee. *(Pause.)* My love is like a Big Fat tree. And not much like a Bumblebee. *(Crumples paper and tosses it away.)* Who am I kidding? It's too nice today, anyway. Why can't I just sit in the park like a normal Human Being and look relaxed. **(Girlfriend** *enters park.)* Here she comes again! She doesn't even know I exist. What is this strange feeling that comes over me when she is near.

My heart goes Pit-a-Pat, my knees get weak, and I feel like I want to . . . Buy a *Pumpkin! (Pause.)*

Girlfriend: What?

Poet: I mean *Sing!* What's wrong with me?

Spuds O'Malley *(walking by):* You're not sick, you're just in love.

Poet *(to audience):* I'm in love. This must be love, because I feel so bad. *(Runs after* **Girlfriend.***)* Miss. Miss . . .

Girlfriend: What?

Poet: I love you.

Girlfriend: I'm very happy for you. **(Girlfriend** *continues walking off.)*

Poet *(to audience):* There must be more to love than this, kids. Don't you think? *(Goes after* **Girlfriend.***)* Oh, Miss . . . Miss?

Girlfriend: What is it? I'm late for work.

Poet: I won't keep you long. It's just that I want . . . I want . . . *(To audience:)* What is this strange desire that comes over me and expresses itself in *wanting? (Pause. To* **Girlfriend***:)* I want you to be my girl.

Girlfriend *(sighs):* Swell. I'm your girl. *(Exits.)*

Poet: Ah. That's more like it! *(He looks. She is gone.)* And now she's gone. Without a word of Goodbye. These things seldom work out. I think I've found that. *(Pause.)* What am I going to do? I felt so good and now I feel so bad. *(Pause.)* I think I'll end it all. *(Someone brings out a pail of water and places it in front of the bench. The* **Poet** *climbs up on the bench. He composes:)*

Oh, you have treated me so bad I never will forget.
I now am going to drown myself.
And I'll probably get Wet. *(He prepares to jump.)*

Passerby: Hey. You should be a poet.

Poet: I am a poet.

Passerby: Then you should be a better poet. *(***Passerby** *exits.)*

Poet: Sometimes people can be very thoughtless, huh, kids?

*(***Aunt Georgie** *enters.)*

Aunt Georgie *(to audience):* Time passes. *(The* **Poet** *hits her in the face with a pie.)*

Poet: If I want narration I'll ask for it. *(Pause.)*

Aunt Georgie: You gotta nother pie?

Poet: No.

Aunt Georgie: Later that evening. *(Exits.)*

Poet *(sitting on bench):*

City Sunsets make me Blue—
They're so Red and Blue.

I look out into the Blue,
And I do get Blue.

(The Wacko Account Executive *walks by.)*

Uh, Lady . . . Lady . . . ?

Wacko: Yes?

Poet: I'm gonna write you a poem, you're gonna give me some money, huh? Whaddaya say?

Wacko: What do you take me for?

Poet *(to audience):* About sixty smackers, I hope! *(To* **Wacko**:) I take you for a lover of Beauty and Art.

Wacko *(pause):* Okay. Hit me.

Poet: Um . . . Um . . . I have it!

The Night is Cold, the Sky is Dark.
I'd rather be home than out in the Park. *(Pause.)*

Wacko: Is that all?

Poet: Yes.

Wacko: I don't know very much about poetry, but I know it's not very long.

Poet: "Long. Long." What is this babble about "long"? What is this "length" nonsense? It's a *poem. (Pause.)* It's *art.*

Wacko: Okay. How much money do you want?

Poet: Sixty Dollars.

Wacko: Sixty Dollars?! You have got a lot of nerve and Gall! Here's a quarter, it's worth about a nickel. Take it or leave it. *(Hands him quarter.)* Good night. *(Exits.)*

Poet: Nobody appreciates good poetry anymore. Well, a quarter is a quarter, and no other coin can make that statement.

(A **Hippie** *enters.)*

Hippie: Hey, man, got any loose change?

Poet *(absentmindedly):* Here. *(Gives* **Hippie** *quarter.)*

Hippie: Thanks, cheapskate.

(The **Poet** *chases* **Hippie** *offstage.* **Pressman** *and* **Prince** *appear and read out of the* Old Storybook.*)*

Pressman: And so he chased the Hippie, hoping to overtake her and to beat her about the head and shoulders with a Brick. But as she was faster than he . . .

*(***Poet** *reappears, panting.)*

Poet: Lost her. Drat! And *now* what am I ever going to do? That ungrateful girl went off with my whole life savings, and I still need sixty dollars. *(Pause.)* What shall I ever do . . .

Entire Cast *(offstage):* Get a Job!

Poet: A Job? Me? A poet? Work? Toil? Labor? *(To audience:)* Kids, do you know what a poet is? Do you know, kids? Why, he's the man that lays it on the line and sums *up* this whole cockamamie flea market that we call "life," for each and every one of us — to help us live our humdrum, day-to-day and ofttimes fraught-with-pain excursions from the womb to tomb with dignity and strength. Why, kids, he's the guy who . . .

*(***Aunt Georgie** *enters.)*

Aunt Georgie: Dave? Dave? Uh, the cast asked me to ask

you if we maybe could get back to the story. *(Pause.)*
We're running out of time. *(Pause.* **Poet** *glares at* **Aunt
Georgie** *and* **Aunt Georgie** *hits herself in the face with
a pie. Exits. Pause.)*

Poet: Ah! I feel Great! Where were we? Right. A job!
Actually not a bad idea. But where am I going to get
a job at this time of night? *(***Spuds O'Malley*** enters.)* Excuse me, officer . . . ?

Spuds: Let me ask you something, fella. Did you ever
think what it means to have a hankerin' for French Fried
Potatoes and nary a one of 'em in the land? Did ye ever
hear of the Great Patatah Famine? Did ye? And what
do ye think it was *about*?

Poet: Well . . .

Spuds: Patatahs! *None* of 'em! That's right. Nary a patatah to be found for love or nothin'. *(To audience:)* You
talk about discomfort! *(To* **Poet***:)* The Great Patatah
Famine. And where did they hold it? Ireland! That's
right. Why me own poor mother used to set me on her
knee . . .

Poet: Excuse me, officer . . . ?

Spuds: Move along, Bud. *(Starts to exit.* **Poet** *takes a tie
out of his pocket and puts it on.)*

Poet: Excuse me, Officer . . . ?

Spuds: Yes sir. What can I do for you?

Poet: Where could I get a job, now, do you think?

Spuds: Well sir, you might try *(points)* over at the Factory.

Poet: Thank you. *(Takes off tie.)*

Spuds: Move along, Bud. *(Accosts a* **Passerby. Spuds** *exiting.)* Excuse me, sir? Did you ever have a yearnin' for a latke, or some Lyonnaise . . . *(Exits.)*

Poet: Okay. Okay. I'm on to a job, and everything is going to be alright!

(The whole **Cast** *comes onto the stage and transforms it into the factory. Which really doesn't need much more than the safe, a chair, and the high-speed multi-tension fractile lathe.* **Pressman** *and* **Prince** *direct the transformation.)*

Pressman *(exhorting stagehands):* On Prince, on you Huskies.

Prince: Woof Woof.

(At the factory. The **Owner** *is inside.* **Poet** *enters.)*

Owner: We're closed!

Poet: I've come about the job.

Owner: You're late.

Poet: No. I don't work here. I'd like to *get* a job here.

Owner: What do you do?

Poet: Make up poems.

Owner *(pause):* You know anything about a High-Speed Multi-Tension Fractile Lathe?

Poet: That's a tough one, alright. *(Pause.)* Here goes:

The multi-tension Fractile Lathe
Makes life a Joy in many Waythe
It turns at all the highest speeds
And feeds on Electricity!

Among the Tools it has no peer.
It's better than a . . .

Owner: Okay. Shuddup. I tell you what. We need a night watchman. When can you start?

Poet: Right now.

Owner: Swell. You're hired.

Poet: Um. What does it pay?

Owner: Sixty dollars.

Poet: Sixty dollars! Just what I need for my Rent! *(To audience:)* Can you believe this?

Owner: I'm very happy for you.

Poet: Please, when do I get paid?

Owner: Payday is tomorrow morning.

(Aunt Georgie enters in a huff.)

Aunt Georgie *(to audience):* What is this, a *fairytale?* Huh? I mean, I'm no stranger to the *theater*, kids, huh? But this is a little bit much. Come on now. Don't you think? Now, I'm on your side, kids. You come in here . . . You pay good *money* . . . You sit down politely . . .

(Prince sneaks up on her and hits her with a pie. Both exit.)

Poet: Thank you for the job. **(Owner** *starts to exit.* **Poet** *yawns.)* Say. Do you have an alarm clock?

Owner: Sure, right in the . . . HEY! What do you mean, you ninny? You're supposed to stay awake!

Poet: Of course. How gauche of me. *(Waves.* **Owner** *exits.)* Good night. **(Poet** *yawns.)* The day is, apparently, saved.

The day is saved
Because I'm paid!
Tomorrow morn my fortune's made.
I'll guard the lathe . . .

Owner *(re-entering):* I forgot to tell you. No poetry. *(Pause.)* It's a Company Rule.

Poet: Alright. Good night.

(Owner *exits.* **Poet** *goes to sleep.* **Pressman** *and* **Prince** *come on.* **Pressman** *reads from the* Old Storybook.*)*

Pressman: And so he fell asleep.

(Pressman *exits.* **Prince** *stays on.* **Prince** *looks around, the only person on stage is the* **Poet,** *and he is asleep.* **Prince** *delivers some of his own poetry to the audience.)*

Prince: Life:

Life is a dream of Geometry.
Life is a dream of Space.
Life is a dream of some Orient Queen
Who got whacked in the head with a mace.

(Pause. **Prince** *exits. Pause.* **Two Thieves** *enter, sneaking into the factory.)*

Gene: Where's the safe?

Boots: Don't know.

Gene: Any ideas?

Boots: We could look for it.

Gene: Good.

Boots: It's probably around the money. If we find the money the safe will probably be right around it.

Gene *(to audience):* Does that make sense? *(To* **Boots:***)* Just give me your flashlight.

Boots: I forgot it.

Gene: Well, then, give me a match.

Boots: I gave up smoking last week.

Gene: You did?

Boots: Yeah.

Gene: How'd you do it? I've been trying to give it up for eighteen years.

Boots: I just made up my mind and I did it.

Gene: I wish I'd never started.

Boots: Mmm.

Gene: Yeah. If I'd never started it would be a lot easier to give it up. *(Takes out cigarettes.)* Got a match?

Boots: I gave it up.

Gene: Then turn on a light.

(**Boots** *turns on a light. The* **Poet** *wakes up and starts apologizing.)*

Poet: I wasn't really asleep. That is, I *was* asleep, but I wasn't doing it for pleasure. I was having a bad dream. I won't do it again. Ever.

Boots: Take it easy, we don't work here.

Gene: You didn't have to tell him that.

Boots: Well, if you're going to do something you might as well be proud of it. *(To* **Poet:***)* We're thieves.

Poet *(pause):* Really?

Gene: Yeah.

Poet: You mean this is a . . .

Gene: That's right, so don't try to . . .

Poet: Sure. No, no. I wouldn't.

Boots: Good. *(Pause.)*

Poet: Am I allowed to yell for help?

Gene: What do you do here?

Poet: I'm the guard.

Gene: Then what's the point to yell for help? The only one who would come if you yelled is you. And you're already here.

Poet: That's true. *(Pause.)*

Gene: Where's the safe?

Poet: I don't know.

Boots: Tell us, or we'll pump you full of holes.

Poet: It's in the next room. *(The **Thieves** start to exit.)*

Gene: You see? I told you. All you have to do is get a little tough with these guys and . . . *(Stops. To **Poet**:)* What do you mean "the next room"? This is the only room there is.

Poet: I was guessing. *(Pause.)*

Boots: You don't know where the safe is?

Poet: No.

Boots: Why?

Poet: I'm not really the night watchman. I just work here. That is, I just took the job tonight. I *am* the watchman, but I *really* am a poet. I took the job to pay my rent. And if my boss finds out that I was sleeping while you snuck in . . .

Boots: Just a sec. We didn't sneak in.

Poet: No?

Boots: We *broke* in.

Poet: What's the difference? *(Pause.)*

Boots: Semantics.

Poet: Alright. If he finds that I was sleeping while you broke in I'll get fired and I won't be able to pay my rent and I'll get thrown out on the streets.

Thieves *(in unison):* Oh, how sorry that would make me.

Poet *(to audience):* I wonder if behind this tough talk hide two sensitive men who find a life outside the law distasteful and demeaning.

Boots: What's this bozo sayin'? *(Pause.)*

Poet *(to audience):* Probably not.

Gene: Okay. Now tell us where's the safe.

Poet: I *told* you. I'm just some poor poet.

Gene: Prove it. *(Pause).*

Poet: I look like a poet, don't I?

Boots: Everybody looks like a poet these days.

Gene: Rhyme something.

Poet: What?

Boots: Something hard. Rhyme "cactus."

Poet: "Cactus . . . cactus." Gentlemen, I must admit I'm greatly embarrassed, but you happen to have picked the one word in the English Language with which nothing rhymes.

Gene *(pokes* **Poet** *with gun):* Rhyme it!

Poet: Mattress.

Boots *(pause):* Mattress? *(Pause.)*

Gene: It doesn't really rhyme.

Poet: You must admit it's close, though. Matt-*ress* . . . cac-*tus* . . . *(Pause.)*

Oh, I am thorny-pricked from Cactus,
And I must lie on my Mattress, for . . .

Gene: Let's get out of here. *(They exit.)*

Poet *(visited by inspiration):*

For I'd fallen out of Practice
And I've fallen off my horse.

(Looks around. He is alone.) Now maybe I can get some rest. *(Yawns. Falls asleep. The two* **Thieves** *are out in the park.)*

Boots: I lost my hat.

Gene: Where?

Boots: If I knew, then it wouldn't be lost.

Gene: Not necessarily. No. You could of lost it on a bus, and know which bus, but it would still be lost. *(Pause. To audience:)* If a Tree Falls in a Forest, does it make a sound?

Boots: I think I lost it at the factory. *(Spuds comes by on his rounds.)*

Gene: Which factory?

Boots: The one we just broke in to.

Spuds *(walking by):* I heard that, you two! You are under arrest!

Boots: I could use a rest.

Poet *(from inside factory):* So could I. Will you guys please knock it off.

Gene: Ah! Ah! Infringing! Trampling on our liberties. You forgot to advise us that anything we ever say is going to be taken personally and so on.

Boots: Also, this is only a play.

Spuds: By the Great Bear Muffler Shops, you're right! *(To audience:)* You see: many policemen are reasonable. *(To* **Thieves***:)* But you should be ashamed of yourselves. In a country where any man, woman, or child can walk into a grocery store and walk out with a ten-pound bag of the most perfect food on God's Green Earth . . .Why, if my Sainted Mother . . . *(Exits.)*

Boots: Well, getting back to the story *(to audience:)* or the "plot," as it is called in a play. *(To* **Gene***:)* We now must go back to the Factory.

Gene: For what?

Boots: My hat.

Gene: Let's do it, then, and quit this lollygagging.

Boots *(sighs, to audience):* Once upon a time I was a good little boy or girl just like you.

Gene: This is no time to be maudlin, let's go to work. *(They go back into the factory, sneaking about.)* Stop making so much noise.

Boots: Sorry. I can't see the hat. You?

Gene: Use the flashlight.

Boots: I forgot it.

Gene: Well . . .

Boots: I'll turn on the light.

Gene: And draw attention to ourselves?

Boots: Just for a second so I can see where the hat is.

Gene: Alright.

Boots: I just got to find the switch.

Gene: Use the flashlight.

Boots: I forgot it. Wait a sec. Maybe it's in the bag.

Gene: Where's the bag?

Boots: I think I lost it. Can't we just turn on the light one second?

Gene: Just a second.

Boots: Where's the switch?

Gene: Hey. How would I know? Use the flashlight.

Poet: Did you ever hear such nonsense in your life? *(To audience:)* They were better the first time.

Gene: Did you hear something?

Boots: I found it!

Gene: What? The flashlight?

Boots: No.

Gene: The switch?

Boots: No.

Gene: The hat?

Boots: No. The safe!

Gene: Well, that's a start. *(The **Poet** turns on the light.)*

Poet: If you gentlemen are going to keep up this insane conversation any longer I do wish you'd go rob somewhere else.

Boots: Pull your gun on him. *(**Gene** does so.)*

Poet: *I* have a gun, Too!

*(A **Cast Member** runs on stage and hands the **Poet** a gun.)*

Gene: Reach for the sky! *(**Boots**, too, draws a gun, and the three point guns at each other.)*

Poet: Drop it. Don't move, you blackguards.

Boots *(to audience):* I wish *I'd* said that!

Poet: Freeze, you anti-social elements.

Gene: Aha!

Boots: Ohoh!

Poet: Oh, you *would*, would you???

(They all continue to point guns at each other. A phone rings offstage. We hear somebody answering the phone.)

Offstage Voice: Hello? He's on stage. No, I *can't*. He's on *stage*. (Pause.) Oh, alright.

Prince *(comes on stage):* Maurice?

Boots: Yes?

Prince: Phone. *(Exits.)*

Boots: Uh. Excuse me. *(Exits, we hear him talking on the phone, everyone on stage stands around waiting patiently. On phone:)* Hello? I'm working. Around Nine. *(Pause.)* I'm doing a *show*. *(Pause.)* When it's *over*. Okay? Alright, Mother. Goodbye. *(He hangs up and comes back on stage.)* I'm very sorry. *(Everybody assumes their pre-phonecall positions.)* Just don't do anything foolish and you won't get hurt.

Gene: You better do what he says.

Poet: Nobody make any sudden moves. We'll all sit here quietly until the police come. **(Aunt Georgie** *comes out.)*

Aunt Georgie: What tension, kids! What suspense, huh? Conflict! Violence . . . *(***Spuds** *peeks out.)*

Spuds: Potatoes?

Aunt Georgie: No. But Fear and Loathing, Pride and Prejudice, Crime and Punishment . . . Sister Carrie . . . *(Everybody onstage goes off and comes back with a pie.)* . . . The Ugly American . . . Death Comes for the Archbishop . . . *(She turns and sees everybody with a pie.)* Bye, Kids . . .

(She hurries off. Everybody puts his or her pie down, except **Boots,** *who is eating his pie.)*

Boots: Anybody got a napkin? *(He opens the door to the safe.)* Hey, Gene!

Gene: What?

Boots: I got the safe to open. *(He looks in.)* So let's see what's in here . . . books . . . a high-school annual . . . Class of '41 . . . A pumpkin . . . *(Reflectively:)* What

the hell's a pumpkin doing in here? *(The* **Poet** *shrugs.)*
. . . two french-whips . . . hey! Money!!!!!

Gene: Give it to me.

Boots: I just want to count it.

Gene: I'll count it. Thank you. *(Riffles stack of money.)*

Poet: How much?

Gene: One hundred-eighty bucks.

Boots: Yeah? *(Takes money, and starts dividing it.)* Let's
see: you take one; *I* take one *(He continues to count under dialogue.)*

Poet: I didn't realize that they had that much cash around.
I'm going to ask for a raise.

Gene *(pointing gun):* You aren't going to ask for *nothing*,
see?

Boots: *Any*thing.

Gene: You aren't going to ask for anything, see? Because
we don't plan to leave any witnesses.

Poet: Marvellous. I'll be ready in a minute.

Gene: What do you mean?

Poet: I just have to pack my gun and a manuscript or
two.

Gene: What do you mean "pack"? You aren't going anywhere.

Poet: But you just said you didn't want to leave any witnesses.

Boots: Not in that sense, Buddy.

Poet: You mean . . . ?

Gene: Yeah. *(Pause.)*

Poet: Why not just take me with you?

Boots: It's an idea.

Gene: What are you good for?

Poet: I don't quite understand . . .

Gene: What can you do?

Boots: He can rhyme. Any guy rhymes Cactus with Mattress . . .

Gene: Shuddup. What else can you do?

Poet: Not terribly much, I'm afraid.

Gene *(pause):* You ain't got no marketable skills; you're of no use to society, and nobody's gonna miss you if we knock you off.

Offstage Voice: Poetic Justice!

Poet: Wait a second! *(To audience:)* I know I'm going to have to pay for this later. *(To* **Thieves:***)* Why not just make me a member of your gang! *(The* **Thieves** *are taken aback.)* I'm not a criminal by inclination or by training, but I'm sure that I could learn.

Gene: Yeah. You could never learn to be a crook!

Poet: I could!

Gene: I don't believe you.

Poet: No?

Gene: No.

Poet: Oh yeah? How about this, then. How about this: We could take the hundred-eighty dollars from the safe and divide it into three parts. Huh? What's that? An "Inside Job."

Gene *(reflectively):* An inside job . . .

Boots: If we divide it in three parts does that mean we get less or more? *(Back to counting.)* Fifty-four for me and twelve for you . . .

Poet: We each get a little less, but together we get the same amount.

Gene: Well . . .

Poet: *I'm* willing to take a cut.

Boots: Well, ninety-two for me and eight for you . . .

Poet: What do you say?

Gene: But don't you feel you'd be doing the "Wrong Thing"? *(**Aunt Georgie** comes out.)*

Aunt Georgie: What is this, a morality play?

Poet: No, George. It's a legitimate question. Yes. I do feel I'd be doing the wrong thing.

Gene: Well, then, everything's alright. *(Everyone smiles and shakes hands all around, including **Aunt Georgie** who exits. **Gene** to **Aunt Georgie**:)* See you later! *(Both wave.)*

Poet: Alright. Is it a split, then?

Boots: How much do we get?

Poet: Sixty dollars apiece.

Boots: Sounds good.

Gene: Yeah.

Boots: I'm going to buy a car.

Gene: You can't buy a car for sixty dollars.

Boots: Then I'm going to steal a car.

Poet: Speaking of which: do you gentlemen have any plans for a "getaway"?

Gene *(pause):* We thought we'd just . . . leave.

Boots: Yeah.

Poet: Hmm. Simple. Simple and direct. I like it. *(They start to leave.)* Wait a minute—I really should try to get a replacement.

Gene: At this time of night?

Poet: I suppose you're right.

Boots: So, yeah. Come on. Let's beat it.

Poet: No rush. After all, I'm the night watchman. *(The Poet freezes.)*

Gene: What is it?

Boots: Is he dead?

Gene: I don't know.

Boots: Maybe his conscience is bothering him.

Gene: Are you stepping on his toe? *(Boots looks.)*

Boots: No. *(Pause.)*

Gene: This is weird. *(The Poet unfreezes.)*

Poet: Gentlemen! An inspiration! Prompted by my foray into the lower depths of crime: A POEM! "The Night Watchman."

The Watchman — watcher of the night
Recites, re-iterates and Writes
Soliloquies of Watching Thoughts
'Though all his watching come to Naught.
For deep within his Naive breast
The yeast of Treason makes its nest.
(**Spuds** *enters and stands watching the recital.*)
Deceit, the bitterest gall to Joy
Has, heavy-handed, caught the boy
And When . . .
(*The* **Poet** *looks and sees* **Spuds**. *Stops.*)

Spuds: Go on. I like it. (*The two* **Thieves** *turn and see* **Spuds**.)

Gene: The Cops!

Boots: The Fuzz.

Gene: The heat!

Boots: Gendarmes.

Gene: Gestapo.

Boots: John Law.

Gene: Bulls.

Boots: Dicks.

Gene: Flatfeet.

Boots: Pigs!

Spuds: That's not nice.

Boots: . . . sorry.

Gene: You loose your turn. (*Thinks.* **Poet** *whispers to him.*) Bobbies!

Boots: Not bad.

Spuds: Not bad . . . ? Not bad . . . ? You shoulda seen 'em in the streets of Belfast, knee-deep in home fries they was. It was a sight to . . . *(He composes himself.)* By the way. What's going on here? *(***Thieves** *exit.)*

Poet: Officer, I'd like to report a robbery.

Aunt Georgie *(offstage):* Why don't you, then? No initiative. *(She comes out on stage.)* Now, Children. Initiative is what made this country what it is. It is the . . . *(She is whacked out by a huge hammer, or a pumpkin falling on her head, or something, and retreats offstage.)*

Poet: Officer, I *am* reporting a robbery.

Late last night the factory of the Acme Corporation, 1234 Yourstreet, Anytown, U.S.A. was robbed of One Hundred-Eighty dollars by person or persons unknown.

Spuds: And who are you?

Poet: I'm the night watchman.

Spuds: Where were you when this took place?

Poet: Right here.

Spuds: What was your part in the proceedings?

Poet: Sixty dollars.

Spuds: Hmm.

Poet: But they split with my share of it.

Spuds: Hmm. *(Pause.)* You're under arrest. *(***Poet** *sighs.)* Will you come quietly?

Poet: Probably not. *(He declaims:)*

Caught in a trap
Like a Rat. With a snap!
Left for the rap
Without Mercy a scrap.
Caught in the vise of my . . .

(*Generally:*) What rhymes with "vise"?

Spuds: Save it for the judge.

Poet: Oh, how am I ever going to pay the rent?

(*They start to exit.*)

Spuds: Keep moving.

Poet: May I say one thing before I go?

Spuds: Yes.

Poet (*to audience*): Friends, Learn from my example.
If you're not smoking, don't start.
If you *are* smoking, stop.
If you've stopped smoking, continue.
Thank you.

Spuds: Dave, If I could add one thing to that . . . (*To audience:*) Did you know that one medium-sized baking potato has less calories than eighteen ounces of small curd cottage cheese?

(*They go off together.* **Thieves** *come out on stage with rest of* **Cast** *to shift the scene.*)

Boots: Fade out, fade in and the scene is now transported, gentles, to the apartment.

(*Everybody shifts to the scene.* **Pressman** *yelling "Mush," and each to his or her own whim. In the apartment. The* **Landlord** *inside. The* **Girlfriend** *at the door, knocking.*)

Girl: Knock knock knock!

Landlord: That's a nasty cough you've got there!

Girl: No. I'm *knocking*.

Landlord: Check your plugs.

Girl: What?

Landlord: Nothing. *(To self:)* It's a joke. Everybody's funny in this play but me. *(To* **Girl***:)* Come in. *(She does so.)*

Girl: Thank you. I was wondering if maybe you could help me.

Landlord: Sure, Miss. In what special way?

Girl: I'm looking for someone who used to live here.

Landlord: Yeah. The guy upstairs.

Girl: How did you know.

Landlord: It advances the plot. So big deal.

Girl: Do you know where I can find him?

Landlord: Hey, I've got no interest in the fellow. He was a troublemaker, plus he was a poet, and if the rent isn't paid in an hour and a half he doesn't live here any more.

Poet *(offstage):* You mean there's still hope!

Landlord: One hour-thirty minutes.

Girl: Beast!

Landlord: That was uncalled for.

Girl *(to audience):* He's nothing but a fat, capitalistic parasite, Exploiting the Artistic Community and . . .

(**Aunt Georgie** *comes out and talks to the audience.*)

Aunt Georgie: "Stereotyping"! Now, kids, what the Girl-friend's doing . . .

Landlord: That's okay Georgie. I'm proud of it. *(To audience:)* And, plus, it buys the groceries! *(Winks.)*

Aunt Georgie: Suit yourself.

Girl *(exiting):* Money. What a worthless thing to get upset about.

Aunt Georgie: Alright, everybody, to the Jail!

*(Everybody comes out and shifts the scene to the jail. In the jail **Pressman** and **Prince** are playing poker.)*

Pressman: Two pair. Tens over.

Prince: Woof woof woof. (**Pressman** *throws his cards in disgust.*)

Pressman: New deck. New deck.

Prince: Arf.

Pressman: Because I *want* one. Alright?

*(**Spuds** enters with the **Poet** in tow.)*

Spuds: Got a new one for you, Pressman.

Pressman: Hot Beavers, Prince. A criminal!

Prince: Bow Wow.

Poet: Who asked you?

Pressman: Don't be surly, son. The Wheels of Justice grind Show, but Slure. *(Pause. Everybody looks at **Pressman**.)* Your bail is sixty dollars.

Poet: I need sixty dollars to get out of jail?

Pressman: Yes.

Poet: This is ridiculous. I was trying to get sixty dollars when I was arrested.

All: (*save* **Prince,** *who* "Woofs.") That's why you were arrested.

Pressman: Book him, Prince. (**Prince** *hits the* **Poet** *with a book.*)

Prince: Arf.

Spuds: Do you play cards?

Poet: I *have*.

Spuds: Play a little then, son. Take your mind off of your troubles.

Poet: Alright.

Spuds: Play for a little something, just to make it interesting?

Poet: Oh, alright. But you'll have to remind me of the rules if I forget.

Spuds: Sure. (*Produces potato.*) Potato . . . ?

Poet: Thanks.

(*At the factory.*)

Girl: Excuse me, sir, I'm looking for a friend . . . An Acquaintance. Actually, he's my boyfriend.

Owner: What's his name, Miss?

Girl: I don't know.

Owner (*to audience*): Ah, youth!

Girl: He might have come by here last night.

Owner: Well, no one came by here last night except a wand'ring poet who I hired as night watchman, and two thieves.

Girl: What did the poet look like?

Owner: Like a poet.

Girl *(reflectively):* Everyone looks like a poet these days.

Owner: And the three of 'em were in *league* together, don't you know.

Girl: Mmm.

Owner: They planned to rob the Factory.

Girl: Mmm.

Owner: But the two thieves got away.

Girl: Mmm. And the poet?

Owner: He was caught.

Girl: Where is he now?

Owner: Where would you put a poet if you wanted to keep him in one place.

Girl: Library?

Owner: No.

Girl: Bar!?

Owner: No. In Jail, Miss! In the Jail!

Girl: How am I going to pick out one poet out of the thousands in jail . . . ? *(She exits.)*

Owner: Meanwhile, back at the jail . . .
*(Everybody comes on and shifts the scene back to the jail. **Spuds** and the **Poet** are playing cards.)*

Poet: Go fish.

Spuds: You sure you never played this game before.

Pressman: Sit, Prince!

Poet: Never gambled in my life.

Prince: Arf Arf.

Spuds: You sure?

Pressman: Speak!

Poet: Lay you six to five. **(Prince** *lies down.)*

Spuds: Let's try some other game.

Pressman: Drop dead, Prince.

Poet: What would you like to play?

Spuds: What do you know?

Poet: Poker, gin, five hundred rummy, pinochle, canasta, dictionary, Spit in the Ocean, Spit in the Bucket, Spit in the Soup, Spit in the Other Bucket, Authors, Baccarat . . .

Spuds: War?

Poet: You'll have to remind me as we go along.

(The **Girlfriend** *comes up and presents herself to* **Pressman.** *)*

Girl: Pardon me, I'm looking for a friend.

Pressman: This isn't the Salvation Army.

Spuds: She said she's looking for a friend, not a doughnut.

Everybody *(humorlessly):* Ha ha.

Poet: A doughnut, too, can be a friend!

Oh, A cruller in the morning to a feller who's in need
With a steaming cup of coffee is a friend, indeed!
On a cold and rainy evening when you're chilled down
   to the bone,
Get your mitts upon a doughnut and you'll never be alone.

Girl: I have reason to believe he may be in this jail.

Pressman: And why is that?

Girl: I can hear him.

Poet: . . . Oh, Bake them, fry them, glaze them. Oh,
Sugarcoat them, do!

Pressman: Hey, will you knock it off in there?

*(**Poet** stops declaiming.)*

Girl: Can I see him?

Pressman: I suppose so. You carrying any files, saws,
hammers, nailclippers, automatic, semi-automatic . . .

*(As **Pressman**'s list continues **Prince**, simultaneously,
comes forward and gives his poem to the audience.)*

Pressman *(continues):* Lethal or unpleasant and/or thought-provoking matter. Harmful or debilitating drugs, por- or pro-nography, geography, geometry, or Small-scale railroad equipment? *(Draws breath.)*

Prince: The Dog:

The Dog, the Dog.
He lives in the Marsh.
His bark is Mute,
His life is Harsh.

(Pause.)

His paws are wet.

Girlfriend: Anyone ever tell you you're kinda butch?

Pressman: . . . travellers cheques, telephone books, unlicensed barnyard fowl or fishing tackle, magnetos, torpedos, mosquitos, potatoes . . .

Spuds *(looking up from game):* What?

Pressman: Nothing. Gnats and/or other or separate categories of flying, winged or self-propulsive large or small-scale foodstuffs, by-products thereof or intent to do so?

Girl: I . . .

Pressman: Provocative or *décolletée.*

Poet: Is she allowed to bring me an aspirin?

Pressman: I believe so. Why?

Poet: Because you're giving me a terrible headache.

Pressman: I'm just following Official Procedure.

Aunt Georgie: Remember that phrase, Boys and Girls.

Pressman: Oh. Oh, alright. Go in. Heel, Prince.

Prince: Arf Arf. **(Girlfriend** *goes over to the* **Poet's** *cell.)*

Girl: Hi.

Poet: Hi.

Girl: How ya doin'?

Poet: Okay.

Girl: Wanna kiss me?

Poet: Sure. *(He kisses her.)*

Poet: And now, my love . . .

Spuds: Hey . . .

Poet: And now, my dearest . . .

Spuds: Hey . . .

Poet: Light of my life: Whilst Bound in Chains of . . .

Spuds: Hey, save it, will ya? You can always spend time with the women. How often do you get a chance to play cards? *(Pause.)*

Girl: He's got a point.

Poet: Officer, I'm about to plan a daring escape. I need "My Woman's" help. Now, your assistance will be appreciated.

Spuds: Uh uh. I'm losing thirty Dollars in Potatoes to you, Champ. And you aren't going anywhere.

Poet: I really must.

Spuds: Oh, come on. You aren't quitting *winners?*

Poet: Love calls. How can I but answer.

Girl *(to audience):* Ain't love grand?

Spuds: Tell you what. Cut you double-or-nothing.

Poet: Oh. Alright. *(They cut cards.)*

Spuds: Jack.

Poet: King.

Prince: Woof Woof!

Girl: Your name is "Prince."

Prince *(dejectedly):* Woof.

Poet: You owe me sixty dollars.

Spuds: Will you take a check?

Poet: Cash. Speaking of which. I've just made the sixty dollars for my rent, but I still need sixty for my bail, not counting untold thousands for a brilliant and deceptive legal strategy to keep me out of jail.

Offstage Voice: Crime does not Pay!

Spuds: Shows how much *he* knows.

Poet *(sighs):* Ah! Money. Money money money . . . What am I going to do for money?

Girl: What did you do before you were a poet?

Poet: I've been a poet since the beginning of the play.

Girl: Mm. *(Pause.)* I've got an Idea!

Poet: What?

Girl: Well, I *am* the incredibly rich and lovely daughter of a multi-millionaire manufacturer of a common household article known by name to millions of American Homemakers . . .

Poet *(to audience):* I think I love her.

Aunt Georgie *(coming out):* Is this any basis for a meaningful relationship? Seriously, now, kids . . . **(Girlfriend** *hits* **Aunt Georgie** *in the face with a pie.)*

Poet: Thank you.

Girl: . . . so why don't I just *give* you the money?

Poet: I have no idea. *(Pause.)*

Girl: Your foolish pride does not prevent you from accepting such a gift given in the spirit of love and friendship?

Poet: Not a chance.

Girl: Your masculinity is not tied to your financial solvency? You don't confuse cash with potency?

Poet: Nope.

Girl: But, of course, you would insist on prompt repayment of the loan. And interest, as a balm to your self-esteem. *(Pause.)*

Poet: No. *(Pause.)*

Girl: Perhaps you misconstrue me. What I'm saying: You're gonna take this cash from me, sit on your duff, not pay it back, lounge around the bungalow all day long with a handful of "gimme" and a mouthful of "much obliged," well, you can go get stuffed, Jim.

Spuds: With sourcream and chives.

Girl: Pseudo-Bohemian trash! *(Exits.)*

Spuds: Well, how do you like them potatoes?

Poet: If I pay the bail then I can't pay my rent. If I can't pay my rent I've got nowhere to stay. *(Pause.)* Can I pay my bail and then still stay here?

Spuds: No. Why don't you pay your rent?

Poet: Then I'll still be inside cause I can't pay my bail.

Pressman: They've got you inbetween the Devil and the Deep Blue Sea.

Prince: Woof.

(The **Wacko Account Executive** *comes in.)*

Wacko: Hello.

Poet: Hi.

Wacko: Do you remember who I am?

Spuds: Aha! An amnesiac! You know what's good for that? You get a paper bag . . .

Poet: Sure I remember who you are.

Spuds: No. Wait. You hold your breath and count to . . .

Poet: It's okay, Spuds. (*To* **Wacko***:*) You're the lady that I sold the poem to at the beginning of the show.

Wacko: That's right.

Poet: What are you in for?

Wacko: I came to see you!

Poet: You didn't!

Wacko: Yes. I did.

Poet: Why? (*Pause.*)

Wacko: Perhaps it would be simpler if I were to explain it this way: Did you ever see the ad on Television where the woman says: (*Sings.*)

Wacko Products do me good.
I use them every day.
With Wacko Underneath your Hood
You'll never have to saaaaaaay!
Oh, Tow me Away
Please Tow me Away.
My car ran out of Wacko today;
Jaaaaaack me up and make my car Okay
But first Tow me Away!
I did my engine wrong.
Now I must pay.
Tow me, I pray, Away! (*Sotto:*) Tow me away, tow me
    away,
Tow me away, tow me away. Or else I'll have to say:
Oh: Wacko is the Gook for me.

(*Full voice:*)

In Colors Gray and Blue . . .

(*Note: the above, of course, offers a super opportunity for a production number.*)

Poet *(interrupting):* Okay. Okay.

Wacko: You've seen it?

Poet: I don't watch television.

Wacko: Oh. *(Pause.)*

Poet: So?

Wacko: I am the woman responsible for that campaign. I wrote that.

Poet: You wrote that?

Wacko: Yes.

Poet: You're in Advertising?

Wacko: Brigham, Young and Rubicon. *(Pause.)*

Poet: You actually wrote that stuff?

Wacko: I did.

Poet: And you *admit* it? *(Pause.)*

Wacko: The Wacko campaign represents over twenty-one-million dollars annually. We're extremely proud of it at the Agency.

Poet *(sotto):* You can afford it.

Wacko: . . . and I have come here to offer you a position.

Poet: In *advertising?*

Wacko: We were very impressed by your "Night in the Park" at the Agency.

Poet: My poem?

Wacko: Yes.

Poet:

"The Night is Cold, the Sky is Dark,
I'd rather be home than out in the Park"?

Wacko: We feel it represents a new, a vital element—
an honest voice. A young outlook.

Poet: Yeah?

Wacko: And we would like your input on the Wacko
account.

Poet: You want some Wacko Input.

Wacko: Right. You got it.

Poet: You want me to write *advertising?*

Wacko: Yes. And we are prepared to start you at an
annual salary . . .

Poet: Yes . . . ?

Wacko: Oh, say, forty-thousand dollars a year.

Poet: You're kidding.

Wacko: Alright. Fifty thousand.

Poet: No! I'm *pleased.*

Wacko: Alright. Thirty-five.

Poet: No. I was pleased at forty.

Wacko: Alright. Forty.

Spuds: That's a lot of potatoes.

Wacko: Well, what do you say?

Poet *(to audience):* This is a very important moment.
This is a very important decision for me. I'm broke and

friendless and this woman has just offered me a high-paying job with Wacko.

Prince: Woof Woof.

Pressman *(translating):* What's Wacko?

Poet *(to* **Wacko***):* What *is* Wacko? *(Pause.)*

Wacko: We're working on it.

Poet: What?

Wacko: Well, nobody *knows*, exactly. *(Pause.)* It's something for cars.

Prince: Woof Woof.

Pressman *(translating):* What does it *do?*

Wacko: Numerous tests by three leading consumer groups have been unable to determine positively that it does any damage to the engine. *(Pause.)*

Poet: That might be the basis for a jingle:

It doesn't hurt your engine.
It doesn't hurt your *Purse*
It doesn't hurt your . . .

Pressman: Woof Woof.

Prince *(translating):* What do they *make* the stuff out of?

Wacko: Ahh, some special kind of potatoes that they get in Ireland.

Spuds *(becoming apoplectic):* Irish Taties?!?!! *(Has heart attack. Pause.)*

Wacko: What's wrong with him?

Poet: It's a subplot. *(Pause.)* Alright, Ma'am. Now here's what I'm going to do—

(**Gene**, *the thief, enters with a note.*)

Gene: Hey . . .

Poet: Oh, Hi! You're . . .

Gene: Shhhh. I got this note a person asked me to deliver to you. *(Hands him note.)*

Poet: Thank you. (**Gene** *makes "okay" sign and exits.* **Poet** *reading note.)* "Friend. Forgive my hostility. I am afraid I made a fool of myself in the police station. It would never have worked out between the two of us, anyway, as you do not turn me on physically. I was attracted to your great talent. Keep on writing. Let nothing stand in your way. I have paid two years' rent for you on your apartment. Again, I apologize for acting like a silly putzo. Goodbye.

Fondly,
Your Girlfriend." *(Pause.)* "P.S. Please do not read this out loud."

(Pause.)

She paid my rent! She paid my rent!

(**Pressman** *goes over to minister to* **Spuds**.)

Wacko: You're sitting pretty now! That forty grand will be pure profit.

Pressman *(of* **Spuds***):* This man's in shock!

Wacko: What do you say? You could use the money from the job to get you off the hook for the Factory burglary.

Pressman: That's right. You still have to stand trial.

Poet: I know.

Pressman: It's going to go on your permanent record.

Poet: I know, but two wrongs don't make a right.

Boots *(entering): Three* wrongs?

Poet: No. Not even three wrongs make a right. *You* know that. I robbed the Factory, and that was wrong. But selling *Wacko* to an unsuspecting public would not cleanse me of my guilt. No, I'm afraid I'll have to pass on the job.

Wacko: Well, alright. Here's my card, in case you change your mind, and remember: "A Good Engine is a Wacko Engine!" *(Exits.)*

*(****Pressman*** *has opened a can of* Wacko *and is pouring it down* **Spud's** *throat. It seems to revive him.)*

Spuds: Well, what are you going to do now, son?

Poet: I'm going to go home and go to work, Spuds. There's a whole society to be explained out there.

(The whole **Cast** *assembles in the jail for* L'envoi *and the final production number. The* **Poet** *bids adieu to each.)*

Goodbye, Spuds, I'll see you later.
I'll think of you when I eat a tater.

Aunt Georgie, you are quite a guy.
I wish I had another pie.

Sergeant Pressman. Noble Mountie!
The one and only in Cook County.

Goodbye, Prince, you Canine Cutie.
Stick with Pressman, do your Duty.

To my ex-girlfriend, wherever she went,
I just want to thank you for paying my rent.

The story's through, so home I go. *(To audience:)*
I hope you understood the show.

Pressman: Well, Prince, I guess this case is closed.

Prince: Arf and Amen. *(The two* **Thieves** *enter and pull guns and demand that the* **Cast** *"Reach for the Sky.")*

Poet: Hey, you've *gotta* reach for the sky in *this* business!

Cast *(singing):*

Oh, Reach for the Sky
And, Bye and Bye,
Misfortune will Retire.

Today you get whacked
In the Face with A Pie . . .
Tomorrow your pants catch fire . . .

(Big finish:)

Use *Wacko* for your car.

Aunt Georgie *(to audience):* And they all lived as contentedly as possible, under the circumstances, for a reasonable length of time.

The
Frog Prince

The Frog Prince was first presented as a staged reading on May 17, 1982 at The Goodman Theatre, with the following cast:

Emilie Borg, *A Milkmaid*
Linda Kimbrough, *The Witch*
Bruce Jarchow, *The Prince*
Jack Wallace, *A Servingman*

CHARACTERS
The Prince
A Servingman
The Witch
A Milkmaid

SCENE
A Wood

This play is dedicated to Willie

Scene One

Summer. The **Prince**, *gaily attired in a Court Uniform, and his* **Servingman** *are walking through the Wood gathering flowers. The* **Prince** *holds a bouquet. The* **Servingman** *hurries about engaged in the actual picking of the flowers.*

Prince: Huh. I don't think I've ever been in this part of the Forest before. *(Pause.)* It's nice . . .

Servingman: Yes, it is, Sire.

Prince: And what a *day*, huh . . . ?

Servingman: Absolutely, Sire.

Prince: A *day* . . . a *day* . . .

Servingman: . . . an exceptional day.

Prince: Yes. An exceptional day. And a *portentous* day. Enough said about that! You know what I want? A blue flower. Something blue. A touch of blue. I want to tell you something, Bill: what we *need*, what we *need* in life (and *art* is a part of life — and flower arrangement is a part of art — the Japanese have a word for it. Which I've forgotten. It's a two-syllable word. Something like "Kamooka" — a long discipline intended, no doubt, to get you in touch with yourself . . .) What you need in *art*, and what you need in a *bouquet*, in short, is what you need in *life*.

Servingman: And what is that, Sire . . . ?

Prince: Thank you. *Contrast*. Eh? Contrast and balance. Call it Fire and Water. Call it, I don't know, call it *thrust* and equilibrium . . . whatever you call it. You need both of 'em. You need 'em both.

Servingman *(handing him his blue flower):* Your blue flower, Sire.

Prince: . . . who knew this stuff just grew wild . . .

Servingman: . . . for the Fair Patricia . . .

Prince: . . . I mean of course we all know they grow wild. How *else* would they grow . . . ? It's just, you know, you get them at the *florist's*, it's *one* thing. It's a mercantile transaction. You pick 'em out *here* and it's so *personal*.

(Pause.)

Servingman: It is, Sire.

Prince: And you know what *else?* I want to tell you something, Bill: It has an element of *fear* in it. Don't you feel that?

Servingman: I do.

Prince: Hey, you're a cheap date. You know that? But it *does* nonetheless . . . snuffing out a *life* . . . I mean, these things are *breeding* out here. Who knows *why* . . . ? It's awesome. *(Pause.)* Huh? They're so *promiscuous* . . . all the time . . . *who* knows why? Who knows to what purpose they're put here, all the time, feast and famine, liberal, conservative, *they* don't care. They don't care. You know why they don't?

Servingman: Why, Sire?

Prince: Cause they're in tune with *Nature.*

*(An **Old Peasant Woman** walks through the forest near them.)*

Ah! An Old Peasant Woman! Gathering . . . who knows what, huh? Some . . . some *plants* for some herbal *rem-*

edy . . . some, some long lost wisdom, I don't know . . . to cure an aching *tooth*, who knows, some *daffodils* to grace her grandson's *nuptial* bed . . . huh?

Servingman: Yes, Sire.

Prince: . . . for the upcoming day of his Happy Marriage. Just as in *whose* case . . . ? *Exactly.* So you see what's on *my* mind. *(He expatiates on the bouquet he holds.)* A bouquet for my sweet Patricia. Flowers. Picked by Hand. Out of love. For you, My Fair Patricia. *(Pause.)* May we . . . may we in our Married State be closely bound as the *buds* are in this bouquet: Individual, separate, each having its *own* life, and its own destiny . . . but each *united* into something *larger* than itself. By God, I *like* that. I'm going to tell her that when I give her these flowers. You got a pencil . . . ? I swear, walking outside brings out the best in you. *(The* **Servingman** *hands the* **Prince** *a pencil. The* **Prince** *starts writing down his encomium.)* I think it's something like a carburetor: You got to get the air in you to burn the fuel correctly.

Servingman: Sire —

Prince: What?

Servingman: Would Your Highness like someone to gather daffodils to grace Your Highness' Nuptial Sheets?

Prince: Yes, I would, Bill. I would. But it would have either to be a spontaneous *gesture*, eh? Arising out of an *impulse*, eh? *Unheralded* on someone's part . . . an, let's say, an *artistic impulse*, a spontaneous impulse on the part — excuse me here — but it would of necessity need be someone of my own *class*, don't you think? Or it would be puhrutty pre*sump*tive, don't you think? *Or, or* . . . see what I'm saying, if someone in my own class, through an excess of *zeal* got thrown back to some, some atavistic *thing. Or, or* it would have to be, say, if it were a *ritual* the *peasants* had. Do you know what I mean — which ones are the daffodils? *(Bill shows him.)* They're nice. I like them. Yes. If it were an old *ritual*, and, gosh, I don't know . . . if the *peasants*, out of *joy* at the Plighting of my Troth (whatever *that* may mean . . .) eh? To The Fair Patricia, out of jubilation at the uniting of our Kingdoms, and the implied *peace*, good *humor* and *prosperity*, so on, that that may bring; if they dug deep into their past and came up with this custom *just for us.* To make us feel a *part* of things . . . what do you think? Or out of raptures at her beauty. They could do that. That could happen . . .

Servingman: Sire; The Fair Patricia is possessed of beauty bordering on the Ideal . . . the more so for that it shines from within.

Prince: Yeah. And she's a good kid, too. Don't you think?

Servingman: Yes. I do, Sire.

Prince: No. Tell me seriously.

Servingman: No, I do.

Prince: You aren't just *saying* that . . . ? I mean, *you're* gonna have to live with her, too. *(Pause.)* Bill . . . ? Well, *I* think she's exceptional. What do the *People* think?

Servingman: They love her as yourself.

Prince: They love her as myself, they do?

Servingman: They've taken her *completely* to their hearts.

Prince: Yeah? I couldn't get an honest opinion out of you with a Smith and Wesson . . . just kidding. You're a pal, and I appreciate it. *(The* **Peasant Woman** *walks near to them.)* Madam! (What do they say . . . ?) Mother! Good Mother . . . *(To* **Bill***:)* Oh! Oh! Oh! I got it! I got it! You don't know me. You don't know me. Okay . . . ? *(To* **Peasant Woman***:)* Hola, Good Mother! And how doth the day find you? And what a *lovely* day it is! *(Pause.)* I'm but a traveler from Across the Forest who's come here seeking to ply his trade and better his lot. What news is hereabouts? *(Pause.)* What occurrences of note? *(Pause.)* What's in the air, if you get my drift? Uh . . . rumors of the *Court* . . . ? *(Pause.)* Royal *Marriages* . . . That sort of thing . . . didn't I hear the *Prince* was getting married? Which, as we all know, must needs affect us all . . . What sort of a guy is he? And how do the countryfolk take to his fiancée, who I have heard is called the Fair Patricia . . . ?

Peasant: Are those flowers for me?

Prince: Um, *no.*

Peasant: But you have picked them in my field.

Prince: I have?

Peasant: Yes.

Prince: Well. Okay. It's actually not *your* field. It's part of the boundary of the Royal Wood, but if you feel I've trespassed on some *land* you, by "usage," have come to view as *yours,* I understand.

Peasant: Are they for me?

Prince: No. I've *told* you.

Peasant *(pause):* Who are they for?

Prince: A friend of mine, what's it to you?

Peasant: I want them.

Prince: Tough.

Peasant: Give them to me.

(Pause.)

Prince *(to* **Servingman***): She's* a rare old bird — *(To* **Peasant***:)* Well, you know, I *would* give 'em to you, I would, but I made a *promise* over them. I, I made a sort of, they're for someone *close* to me. I made a sort of a little *prayer* over them. Now, if you like, my friend will *pick* you some? Would you like that? Bill . . . ? *(To* **Peasant***:)* How is that?

Peasant: Those flowers must be an offering.

Prince: Well, they are, sort of.

Peasant: For me.

Prince: No, I can't do that. I've told you that. Bill! Give the Good Woman a coin. *(To* **Peasant***:)* Go buy something nice.

Peasant: Those flowers you must offer me, or you will dwell in misery.

Servingman: See here: You have just broken the law. You have Threatened and Insulted . . .

Prince: It's okay. Bill, Bill . . . Alright. *(To* **Peasant***:)* Look. Look here: I've been kind of joking around. *Actually* I'm the Prince. It's alright. I'm not mad at you. I picked the flowers for my Betrothed. The Fair Patricia. Alright? And I said a sort of silly little *prayer* over them that the F.P. and I would be happy. *(Pause.)* Now would you *really* want me to go and give these flowers to someone else? Now? Knowing who they're for? *(To* **Servingman***:)* Give her the money . . .

Peasant: Those flowers you must offer me, or you will dwell in misery.

Prince: Okay, now that's not funny anymore. I'm understandably all *full* of things these days and I'm very *suggestible* and susceptible. Alright? To all sorts of malevolent *influences* and *suggestions* so you just take back what you said. Okay? I'm not *giving* you the flowers, and unless you retract your curse I'm going to throw your tush in jail. Can I make it more clear than that? *(Pause.)* Eh? *(Pause.)* Alright! Well, that's fine! No? *(Pause.)* Bill? I think that I've had enough fresh *air* today . . . when we get back I want her taken *care* of. Get it? In fact, you hurry back and tell the Captain of the Guard I got an *errand* for him. He'll know what I mean. *(The* **Prince** *starts off with the* **Servingman**. *Sotto:)* Just kidding. Thought I'd throw a little *scare* into her. *(To* **Peasant:**) And one last thought I'd like to leave you with: *Monarchy* . . .

Peasant: Those Flowers you must offer me, or you will dwell in Misery.

Prince: You're pushing your luck, Babe. *(Pause.)* You really are, and you just wait 'til these big *brawny* types get down here with their *pickaxes*, you're gonna be whistlin'a different *tune*. You see there's such a thing as *civility* . . .

Peasant: Those flowers . . .

Prince: I'm not going to *give* you the flowers . . .

(A big flash. The **Prince** *is changed into a frog.)*

Peasant: You shall remain in this vile form until a pure and honest woman of her own free will shall plant a selfless kiss upon your lips. At that time you shall be restored, but should you tell her of your former state you shall remain a frog forever. Sic Transit Gloria Mundi. You should never have come into my part of the forest.

Scene Two

Fall. The **Prince** *(now a frog) and a* **Milkmaid**.

Prince: I really appreciate your spending this time with me.

Milkmaid: I like you.

Prince: Well, I like you, too, as a matter of fact I like you a lot. I like you more the more I *see* you and you tend to *grow* on me. I think you're smart. I think you're smart and pretty, now what do you think about that — are you susceptible to flattery? *(Pause.)* I know, we all are, everybody likes to be told nice things about themselves, you know what *else* I like about you. You're *generous*. That's something in today's world. Isn't it? It's a *lot*: I think it's rather a *lot*. Not to be . . . *judgmental*, not to be "stuck-*up*" . . . to say, "however 'lowly' someone is, I'm going to see the *good* in them." *You* do that, and I think it's admirable. *(Pause.)* I do.

Milkmaid: You're funny.

Prince: Ah, gedouddahere . . .

Milkmaid: No, you *are*.

Prince: Well, *thank* you.

Milkmaid: You say funny things.

Prince *(pause):* Gee, you're swell.

Milkmaid: You always *flatter* me . . .

Prince: It's just the truth. It's nothing but the *truth*, here you are, *working* every day, working so *hard*, carrying *milk* the whole time . . . uh, carrying *hay*, you look so *pretty* working in the Sun . . . I see you walking *by* . . . you *do* something to me, and Grace . . . can I call you Grace?

Milkmaid: Yes.

Prince: *Grace*, you *do* something to me. Every day I see you going past a *feeling* has grown in my breast, and, Grace, I want to ask you something . . .

Milkmaid: What?

Prince *(sotto):* Okay, here it goes. I choose and elect this woman. And if she will give me all her selfless Love as evidenced by the physical evidence of her giving me a kiss I will be Free. And I choose her. *(To the* **Milkmaid***:)* Grace: I'd like to give you a kiss. Would you give me a kiss? *(Pause.)* Grace . . . ? Would you do that?

(Mourning bells sound.)

Milkmaid: Aren't those bells sad . . . ?

Prince: Did you hear what I said . . . ?

Milkmaid: What? I'm sorry? Wait, I, when I hear those bells, I'm so . . . I suppose that we all have to die. *(Pause.)* And I suppose it's good to be reminded of it. But it makes me sad. They say he was a good man. *(Pause.)* Who's to know? It's hard to know what Great people are, if they're real at all. What qualities they have. I'll tell you what I know. It's sad he died when he was going to wed.

(Pause.) Life is such a mystery. What do you think happened to him?

(Pause.)

Prince: I don't know what you mean.

Milkmaid: The *Prince*. Our Prince who disappeared on his *Wedding* day.

Prince: What happened to him?

Milkmaid: Yes.

Prince: I'm sure that I don't know.

Milkmaid: Maybe it's better. *(Pause.)* Maybe it is. Gone two months and his fiancée is marrying his cousin. *(Pause.)* Life is so strange. I'm sure we love the trials of the Great in that they save us from experiencing them ourselves. *(Pause.)* I suppose that we think they're *more* than us. They can *bear* them. *(Pause.)* That they are *stronger*, or *better (pause)* or *worse* . . . *(Sighs.)* I'll tell you what I think, though.

(Pause.)

Prince: And what is that?

Milkmaid: It's *wrong* to hold a funeral for him today and for his fiancée to wed tomorrow. *(Pause.)* I don't think that that's right.

Prince: You don't?

Milkmaid: Even if she did not love him. *(Pause.)* She could be true to his memory. *(Pause.)* Or she could show respect by being true to the appearance. *(Pause.)* That's what I think. My father says she's doing it to keep the fortune. His cousin inherits today and tomorrow she will wed. I pity the new prince. I do. Life is so tenuous. You can't buy loyalty. It's so good to be loved for yourself. That's something that cannot fade.

Prince: I, look, look, look, I want you to . . . Will you give me a kiss, I really want to kiss you, would you do that?

Milkmaid: Oh, I couldn't.

(Pause.)

Prince: You're disgusted, fine. I disgusted you. All you are is fine talk, when it comes down to *cases* you only care what's on the outside.

(Pause.)

Milkmaid: I hurt you.

Prince: Huh . . .

Milkmaid: I'm sorry. No. Please understand.

Prince: I understand *completely*, you're like all the rest.

Milkmaid: I could only kiss a man I was pledged to marry.

Prince: Will you marry me?

Milkmaid: You're speaking so hastily.

Prince: No, I'm not. I mean it. I will *marry* you. I mean it. I've . . . from my soul . . . now. We'll get married today. I'll take care of you. You won't regret it, I promise you. Someday you're going to look back and remember I said this to you. Will you be mine?

(Pause.)

Milkmaid: I am deeply touched.

Prince: Yeah. You aren't touched. I *know* this pream-
ble. You're *hurt*. You're *appalled*, that I would *presume*
on our *acquaintance* . . . a mere . . .

Milkmaid: I am *touched*. I never will forget this moment. *(Pause.)* I never will forget it.

(Pause.)

Prince: You could learn to love me.

Milkmaid: I love another.

Prince: . . . I have many qualities, and you bring them
out *in* me, that *no* one has seen. I could *learn* from you,
and you could learn to love *me* . . .

Milkmaid: I love another.

(Pause.)

Prince: I'm sorry . . . ?

(Pause.)

Milkmaid: I love another.

Prince: Oh. *(Pause.)* Oh. *(Pause.)* Oh. *(Pause.)* Fine.
That's fine. Getting there a little after the barn *door* was
open, all the *horses* left, I'm shutting up to close the *door*.
Ha. Ha.

(Pause.)

Milkmaid: . . . you're hurt.

Prince: "You love another . . ." never mentioned *that*
. . . some *other* guy . . . well, why don't you go marry
him, then, if you're so "in love" the whole time. Why
don't you do *that* . . . ?

Milkmaid: We have no money. *(Pause.)* I'm going to go.
I want to see the Prince's Funeral.

Prince: Oh, whattaya going to see his "body"? They don't even *have* a body . . . they don't have anything, just a bunch of cheap sentiment, cheap, tawdry, false emotions. Well, maybe that's where you belong . . .

Milkmaid: You're hurt.

Prince: No, I'm not hurt.

Milkmaid: We'll still be friends.

Prince: Oh. We will.

Milkmaid: This was hard for you. I'll always remember that you asked.

Prince: Swell. Tell your boyfriend, too. I'm sure that he'll be touched.

Milkmaid: I'll see you tomorrow.

Prince: Wait. Wait a second. Wait. Hold on. You can't get married 'cause you have no money.

(Pause.)

Milkmaid: No.

Prince: If you *had*, if you could *find* the money you'd get married.

Milkmaid: Yes.

Prince: Okay now, okay now, okay, now, *great*. If someone could — what is it you need, a *dowry*, something like that . . . ? How much do you need?

Milkmaid: Twenty-five Gold Coins.

Prince: Twenty-five Gold Coins, great . . .

Milkmaid: . . . to buy my fiancé out of his apprenticeship.

Prince: Yeah. Yeah. Fine. If someone could *help* you to marry, if someone could *find* you that money, I don't mean to sound *crass*, but if someone *got* you that money, what would you *do* for that guy?

Milkmaid: I'd be eternally in his debt.

Prince: That's good enough for me. Okay! Go on, I'm not going to hold you up, you run along. I don't want you to worry about a thing.

Milkmaid: Oh, I'm not worried.

Prince: You aren't?

Milkmaid: No. I think that Love will find a Way. *(Pause.)* See you tomorrow!

Prince: You bet your boots you will.

(Prince whistles. Servingman appears. Pause.)

Servingman: Sire? *(Pause.)* Sire . . . ? Did she . . .

(Pause.)

Prince: What? Oh. No. No go. Not at all. She won't go for it.

Servingman: But did Your Highness elect her the one who must bestow the kiss?

Prince: Yes. Yes. I did. *(Pause.)* We're committed. *(Pause.)* We're in it, now . . . We're in a little bit of a *quandary (pause)*, but I think I can pull it out.

Servingman: Sire: if we don't pull it out by tomorrow you will be pronounced dead, your fortune will devolve on your Cousin Charles, he will marry the Fair Patricia . . .

Prince: . . . and I'll be Broke and Friendless the rest of my life, yeah, I'm *talking* about fixing it before tomorrow, I'm talking about fixing it right *now*, can you believe the gall of this broad, dead two months, dead two months, dead two months, not *even* dead, what am I *talking* about, I'm right *here* . . . and she's marrying someone else.

(Pause.)

Servingman: It must be very difficult for you.

(Pause.)

Prince: Yeah. Yeah. *(Pause.)* We're going to pull this one off yet. Here's what I want you to do. Go to the Palace. Alright? In the *library* of my *study* on the top *shelf* facing the *windows* there's a Big Blue Book. Alright? It's hollow. Now. We got a little *getaway* money in there, so be careful bringing it back. That was needless. I'm sorry. I know that you'd be careful. *(Pause.)* Bring it back, *tonight* we'll go to the *milkmaid's* house, we'll give her a dowry she'll never forget, she'll kiss me out of gratitude, we hop on back to the Castle, put the kibosh on this whole affair, I save my *fortune*, put the Fair Patricia on a *bus* (you best believe it) and it's *business* as *usual* back at the Old Stand. *Okay*. Let's *do* it.

Servingman: I'm on my way, Sire . . .

Prince: And, hey, and how would you like to be the *Earl* of somewhere . . . ?

(Pause.)

Servingman: I . . .

Prince: Let's not count our chickens, all I want to tell you, it hasn't gone unnoticed what you've done for me.

Servingman: I . . .

Prince: We'll celebrate later. Okay, you better hit the bricks.

Servingman *(exiting):* Your Servant, Sire . . .

Prince: . . . I mean, you can't go around feeling *sorry* for yourself the whole time. The Going Gets Tough, The Tough Get Going. *(Pause.)* Now I've stopped *moping* and we're gonna set a couple of things *straight* around this place.

Scene Three

Winter. The **Servingman** *(in rags) and the* **Prince** *(as a frog) sitting around a campfire. The* **Prince** *reading a newspaper . . .*

Prince: Here's a good one. Woman about five miles from here arrested for not paying the Milk Tax. Five years in prison. "'What will Happen to my Babes' Mom says." Well, that's the Fair Patricia for you . . .

Servingman: Yes, Sire . . .

Prince: Anything for a laugh. You warm enough?

Servingman: Yes. Thank you, Sire.

Prince: "Worst winter in 200 years" well, these things always seem to coincide. Don't you think? Hard times and Hard Weather? *(Pause.)* You know what I think? I think it's sunspots. That's what I think it is. *(Pause.)* You doing okay? Bill . . . ? You okay? I know it's easier for me. I don't eat much. I have cold blood. You got to keep *warm*, and you need a little *protein* once in a while.

Servingman: I'm okay, Sire.

Prince: Here's a good one, "Her Radiance the Fair Patricia and Prince Charles off for extended Foreign Tour. Thousands Cheer . . . " And I don't blame them. Good Riddance to Bad Rubbish. Oh. Here's a happy note! "Parliament endorses emergency Discretionary Powers for Bailiffs." *(Sighs.)* Whaddaya know about that . . . *(The* **Prince** *looks up from his paper.)* Yep. Looks like they're gonna make the *trains* run on time. You okay, Bill . . .?

Servingman: Yes, Sire.

Prince: You don't look well.

Servingman: I'm fine, Sire.

Prince: You got a fever?

Servingman: No, Sire. Not at all.

Prince: Hey, look, Bill, I've been thinking, you don't have to call me "Sire" anymore. *(Pause.)* Okay? *(Pause.)* I mean, these are new times, we have to change with them.

Servingman: The old times will return, Sire.

Prince: Somehow I don't think so.

Servingman: I've never ceased to hope.

Prince: Well, Hope is a wonderful thing, but *reasonably* they've changed the locks on us at the Palace, Fair Patricia's issued a dictum anyone *resembling* The Late Prince was to be shot on sight for defamation of my sainted memory—*she* don't fool around—it's a crime to be seen wearing my *emblem*, and she's got the whole place pretty well cowtied. It looks like Under New Management. That's what *I'd* say.

(Pause.)

Servingman: I've never ceased to hope.

Prince: Well, you hope, but keep it silent, cause if you hope out *loud* it's El Biggo Sleepo, if you follow me, and I'd rather have you around.

Servingman: Thank you, Sire.

Prince: No, it is I who thank *you*, Bill. *(Pause.)* It's I who am in your debt constantly and I am never not mindful of that. You've cared for and protected me with everything at your disposal, and the only coin with which I can repay you is my constant thanks. *(Pause.)* Thank you.

(Pause.)

Servingman: Sire! Here she comes!

Prince: And *some*day, I'm gonna get that broad to *kiss* me, and then we're going to saddle up and *blow* this joint, and go down somewhere *warm*! **(Milkmaid** *enters.)* . . . and we're gonna start a *shoe store* or something. *(To* **Milkmaid***:)* Hi! *(Pause. To* **Servingman***:)* She doesn't look so good today. *(To* **Milkmaid***:)* Hi! Kiddo! Hi! How are you, why don't you sit *down* a spell. Hey, Grace . . . *(To* **Servingman***:)* Get her a *log* or something . . . **(Servingman** *does so. She sits.)* That's better! *(To* **Servingman***:)* What have we got to eat? *(To* **Milkmaid***:)* You look pale as a sheet . . . **(Servingman** *brings broth.)* Some *broth* . . . ? You want some nice *broth* . . . ? *(They feed her.)* Yeesssss. *That's* better . . . ! *That's* better . . . ! Yessssssss. Now: what's the *matter* with you, letting yourself get so run *down* and all . . . ! And how come we don't *see* you anymore . . . you alright? You okay . . . ?

Milkmaid: They took everything.

Prince: Who took everything?

Milkmaid: The Bailiff.

Prince: What did they take? What?

Milkmaid: My fiancé . . .

Prince: . . . yes?

Milkmaid: Could I have some more broth . . . ?

Servingman *(serving her):* My pleasure.

Milkmaid: Thank you. *(Pause.)* Thank you. My fiancé made a remark against The Fair Patricia. *(Pause.)* He was turned in. They took his farm. They came to my farm and they took my cow.

Prince: They took your cow?

Milkmaid: And, yes, and they, he's gone. They put a price on his head. Fifty Golden Coins. Dead or Alive.

Prince: Where is he gone?

Milkmaid: Gone away. He left the country in the night. He left me a note. *(Hands note to the* **Prince.***)*

Prince *(reads):* "Don't worry."

Milkmaid: . . . and they took my cow.

Prince: Who took your cow . . . ?

Milkmaid: I'm basically not a political person . . . I'm going to town to plead my case before The Fair Patricia . . .

Prince: . . . she's out of town . . .

Servingman: Why did they take your cow?

Milkmaid: They said that I was an Accessory.

Prince: What is it that your boyfriend said that got them so ticked off?

Milkmaid: Someone was talking about The Fair Patricia and he said "Handsome is as Handsome Does." I'm going to ask them for my cow back. Do you think that's disloyal to him . . . ?

Prince: No. And I don't think it's gonna get you your *cow* back, either. As a matter of fact, I wouldn't go in there at all.

Milkmaid: . . . I have to eat . . .

Prince: They're going to ask you where he is.

Milkmaid: I won't tell them.

Prince: You won't tell them . . . you *know* where he is?

Milkmaid: No.

(Pause.)

Prince: Somehow I don't believe you.

Milkmaid: I won't *tell* them, though. I'll say I don't know where he is. How will they know?

Prince: You've got a face like a transparent book, for starters. This is no good.

Milkmaid: It wasn't right of them to take my cow.

Prince: It certainly was not.

Milkmaid: What *right* do they have?

Prince: Only force.

Milkmaid: Isn't there any *law* anymore . . . ?

(Servingman produces a golden sword from under his ragged cloak.)

Prince: What's that?

(Pause.)

Milkmaid: Is that *gold* . . . ?

Prince: Yeah. It's gold. But what is it *doing* here, if you get my meaning, when everything *like* it should have been buried *months* ago . . .

Servingman: This is my sword.

Prince: Now, Bill, don't be silly, how could that be *your* sword? When it's festooned all over with the blazonments of Our Late Prince, the ownership of which emblem is *Death?* I'm sure you must have *found* it somewhere, and are going to *bury* it. Immediately . . .

Milkmaid: . . . how did you get that sword?

Servingman: I'm taking it to town.

Prince: Now, that's the dumbest thing I ever heard . . . why would someone unless he didn't want to live anymore *do* a thing like that?

Servingman: I'm taking it to the Goldsmith to be melted down, and with the proceeds I am buying this Young Lady food. In fact I'm buying her a *cow* . . . and some new *clothes* . . .

Milkmaid: No, you can't do that, if they catch you on the *road* with it . . .

Prince: . . . have you been carrying that thing the whole time?

Servingman: It has been my Great honor to.

Milkmaid: No, you can't do that. Thank you, no. It's much too dangerous . . .

Servingman: Farewell.

Prince: I forbid you to go.

Servingman: In what capacity?

(Pause.)

Prince: As your *friend* . . .

Servingman: And as your friend I beg your understanding for my so precipitous departure. Farewell. *(He exits; pause.)*

Milkmaid: I can't believe he's doing that for me. *(Pause.)* I can't believe he's doing this.

Prince: Well, these are hard times, and I think he feels that we all have to stick together.

Milkmaid: Your friend is a very good man.

Prince: Yes. He is.

Milkmaid: What will we do if he doesn't come back?

Prince: I don't know.

Milkmaid: He's got a lot of Pride, hasn't he?

Prince: Yes. He has.

Milkmaid: Is that a good thing?

Prince: I don't know. *(Pause.)*

Scene Four

Spring. The **Prince** *(as a frog) is gathering flowers. He holds a bouquet.*

Prince:

A Blue Flower's best for Spring.
A Blue Flower's best for Spring,
When Ground is raw. *(Pause.)*
Red is the Color of Lust . . .

(To himself:) Well, that's true. Can blue be the Color
of Lust? No, I don't think so. Perhaps some perverted
blue, some *violet* midnight blue . . . some *midnight*
blue, perhaps, it probably depends a great deal on what
surrounds it. *(Pause.)* Bill—I wish you were around to
hear this. 'Cause I think you would appreciate it. *(He
goes over to his journal and writes in it.)*

"A Blue Flower's Best for Spring,
When ground is raw . . .
Red is the Color of Lust . . . "

(The **Milkmaid** *appears, watches him.)*

"Red is the Color of Lust . . . of Saline life, of blood
. . . " well, we know red is the color of blood . . . that's
not very good . . . What other flowers do we have around
here? *(He turns; sees* **Milkmaid.***)*

Milkmaid: Hello.

Prince: Oh, Hi! Oh, wait a minute, will you . . . "Red
is the Color of Lust, of Saline Life . . . of Arrogance and
Sloth; but *Blue* . . . "

Milkmaid: . . . are you writing a poem . . . ?

Prince: . . . hold on a second . . . "*Red* is the color of
pride, and *blue* of loyalty." *(Pause.)* Um . . .

(Pause.)

Milkmaid: . . . did I break your train of thought?

Prince: It's alright. *(Pause.)* It's alright. How are you? I'm sorry. My mind was somewhere else for a second. How are you? I haven't seen you in a while.

Milkmaid: No.

Prince: What have you been doing?

Milkmaid: I've been trying to farm.

Prince: You have.

Milkmaid: Yes. I was getting the farm ready for planting.

Prince: But they took your horse.

Milkmaid: I laid out a small patch behind the hut. *(Pause.)* How have you been?

Prince: I been okay. I was, you know, I was unwell for a time there . . .

Milkmaid: Yes, I know . . .

Prince: . . . since my . . .

Milkmaid: Yes, I know . . .

Prince: . . . since my *friend* died . . . *(pause)* but I'm alright now, I think.

(Pause.)

Milkmaid: What were you doing just now? You were writing a poem.

Prince: Just now. Yes.

Milkmaid: I didn't know that you could write.

Prince: Well, I've been working at it.

Milkmaid: You were writing it for *him?*

Prince: Yes. (*Pause.*) Yes. I was. (*Pause.*) I was picking some *flowers* to take over to his grave, and some thoughts came to me. (*Pause.*) Well!

Milkmaid (*hands him a package*): I brought you this.

Prince: Thank you. What is it?

Milkmaid: My heavy shawl.

Prince: You brought me your shawl?

Milkmaid: Yes. I thought that you could make a little, you could make a *nest* for yourself.

Prince: But *you'll* need it. Next winter . . . You'll surely need it.

Milkmaid: I'm going away.

(*Pause.*)

Prince: You're going away.

Milkmaid: Yes.

(*Pause.*)

Prince: Where?

Milkmaid: I'm going South. I got a letter from my fiancé. He wants me to *join* him.

(*Pause.*)

Prince: Then you must go.

Milkmaid: I (*pause*) I wanted to *ask* you if you would like to *come* with us.

(*Pause.*)

Prince: To come with you to the South.

Milkmaid: Yes.

Prince *(pause):* That's very good of you.

Milkmaid: We would be glad to have you. There would be a place for you.

Prince: That's very good of you. That's very good of you, indeed.

Milkmaid: Will you come?

Prince *(pause):* You want me to come with you and live with you.

Milkmaid: Yes.

Prince: You know, you're a good woman. *(Pause.)* I've wanted to tell you that for a long time. *(Pause.)* And your fiancé's a lucky man. A very lucky man to have someone as loyal as you. *(Pause.)* And as good as you. *(Pause.)* And there's something else, there's something that I'd like to say. I owe you an apology.

Milkmaid: You don't owe me.

Prince: Yes. I do, though. I've, uh, you know, when I *met* you . . . when I *met* you . . .

Milkmaid: That's, that's long ago . . .

Prince: Yes, I think that it is, and do you remember . . .

Milkmaid: You don't have to talk about that if . . .

Prince: No, I want to.

Milkmaid: I know that you were *hurt* that I *refused* you . . .

Prince: Yes, I was.

Milkmaid: If I were *free* . . .

Prince: I was hurt. More im*por*tantly . . .

Milkmaid: If I were *free* your offer would not have been *refused. (Pause.)*

Prince *(pause):* Thank you. *(Pause.)* Thank you very much. I . . . thank you very much. I . . . *(Pause.)* You would have married me? *(Pause.)*

Milkmaid: Yes.

Prince: I'm honored.

(Pause.)

Milkmaid *(starting to go):* Well . . .

Prince: Wait, please, I wanted to *say* . . . I wanted to *say* when I first *knew* you I, I think, I wanted, there was something I *wanted*, I *wanted* to take advan . . .

Milkmaid: Shhh.

Prince: To, no, to take . . .

Milkmaid: . . . it's alright.

Prince: . . . to take *advantage* of you. *(Pause.)* There. *(Pause.)* There. And *further*more, however I've *changed* has in large part been because of you, and Bill, of course, but because of you. Okay. I'm through. Enough. Okay. I've said it. There. I apologize. It came out a bit creepy but I mean it. *(Pause.)*

Milkmaid: Will you come with me?

Prince: I . . .

Milkmaid: Will you come with me to the South? And live with us?

Prince: I . . . *(Pause.)* I . . . *Thank* you. But I don't think that I can. *(Pause.)* I think I'll stay here.

(Pause.)

Milkmaid: It will be cold here.

Prince: Yes. *(Pause.)* I . . . Yes, it will, but . . .

Milkmaid: . . . you have *ties* here.

Prince: Yes. *(Pause.)* But thank you for asking me.

Milkmaid: I have to go. I want to cross the border before it gets dark. They close it down.

Prince: You have a safe trip.

Milkmaid: I'll think of you.

Prince: I'll think of you, too. I wish, I wish there was something I could *give* you . . . to *think* of me.

Milkmaid: Oh, I won't forget you.

Prince: I . . . isn't it funny; I was looking for a "jewel" or something to give you. Hah. Haha. I don't even have a *pocket*! Hah! Isn't it funny how some things take us back.

Milkmaid: What do you mean?

Prince: I was thinking of my Old Friend. I must have been thinking of him, and it took me back to another time. *(Pause.)* Do you think we never know the good things 'til they've passed?

Milkmaid: I don't know.

Prince: I've been thinking that.

(Pause.)

Milkmaid: You have a good heart.

Prince: Do I? Thank you. You do, too. Thank you. Oh. Oh. *(He starts writing.)* "Red for Pride, Blue for Loyalty . . . a good heart's *red* . . . a good heart's red . . ."

Milkmaid *(softly):* Goodbye . . . *(She kisses him and slips quietly away.)*

Prince: "A Good Heart's red . . . " Now we need *yellow*, we need some *contrast . . . yellow* . . . Blue . . . *(He changes back into a prince.)* Blue for Spring, red for Saline Lust . . .

(The **Old Peasant Woman** *appears.)*

Peasant: Hello. *(The* **Prince** *looks up; pause.)* Hello.

Prince: What are you doing here?

(Pause.)

Peasant: Hello.

Prince: Yes. Hello. It's been a long time.

Peasant: Look at yourself.

Prince: I know what I look like.

Peasant: Look at yourself.

(The **Prince** *does so; pause.)*

Prince: I seem to have changed. *(Pause.)* Well. *(Pause.)* Yes. *(Pause.)* It's been a long time. Hasn't it? *(Pause.)* Yes. And here you are again. *(Pause.)* And now I have changed back. *(Pause.)* How about that. *(Pause.)* How about that. *(Pause.)* How about that. *(Pause.)* May I ask you something? I'd like to understand. There's something that I've wanted to ask you for so long. The last time that we met . . . may I ask you . . . the last time that we met. I was about to get married. I ruled the kingdom. I refused a request that you made, at that time I thought that I was within my rights . . . I was on Royal Land . . . I was, let us say, on land I *knew* as Royal Land. Even if we were to say that possession of that land was in some form a usurpation. I picked *flowers*. In a moment of exuberance. I felt no ill will toward you. None at all. And I was punished. My love proved false. My kingdom was taken from me. My friends were ruined. My comrade lost his life . . . *(Pause.)* Don't you think I was unduly punished? *(Pause.)* Or was it punishment for some . . . for some general *arrogance*? For my acceptance of the perquisites of *rank*?

Peasant: Are those for me?

Prince: I'm sorry?

Peasant: Those flowers that you hold, are they for me?

Prince: No. *(Pause.)* They're for my friend. *(Pause.)* Who has died. I'm taking them to his grave.

Peasant: You must offer them to me.

Prince: They're for my friend's grave.

Peasant: Those flowers you must offer me, or you will dwell in Misery.

(Pause.)

Prince: They're somewhat *sacred*. *(Pause.)* They're for my *friend*. *(Pause.)* Here. Here they are. *(He gives her the bouquet.)* Take them. *(Pause.)*

Peasant: Thank you. *(Pause.)* They're lovely.

Prince: Yes. They are.

Peasant: I think that they're the loveliest thing in this part of the Wood.

Prince: Yes. I do, too.

Peasant: Thank you for offering them to me.

(Pause.)

Prince: That's perfectly alright.

(She exits. He puts the Milkmaid's shawl over his uniform and starts out of the Wood.)

The Revenge
of the
Space Pandas
or
Binky Rudich
and the
Two-Speed Clock

A comedy

CHARACTERS

Leonard (Binky) Rudich, *a scientist*
Vivian Mooster, *an associate*
Bob, *a sheep*
Mrs. Rudich, *Leonard's mother*
George Topax, *a supreme ruler*
Edward Farpis, *an ex-matinee idol*
Various Space Pandas, Retainers, Jesters,
Announcers, Residents of Crestview, Etc.

TIME: *The present*

PLACE: *The Rudich House, Waukegan,
Earth and Crestview, Fourth World in the
Goolagong System*

"Life is a dream of Geometry,
Life is a dream of Space;
Life is a dream
Of some Orient Queen
Who got whacked in the head with a Mace."
        from *The Poet and the Rent*

Scene One

At rise: **Binky** *is discovered at his attic worktable fiddling around with stuff. His faithful companion,* **Bob, the Sheep,** *is lounging in a corner of the attic reading the paper. The radio is playing.*

Radio: . . . and no relief in sight. We can look forward to high temperatures and sticky, wet humidity right on through the weekend.

Bob *(under his breath):* Great.

Radio: . . . and now the sports . . .

Bob *(turning off the radio):* I sure would like to get out of town this weekend. It says in the paper here that by the year 2000 we will have solved our travel problems altogether.

Binky: Yes?

Bob: It says that we'll just have these pills, and any time you want to go someplace, all that you do is take a pill . . .

Binky: . . . uh huh . . .

Bob: And then you don't want to *go* there anymore.

*(***Vivian*** appears at the tree outside the window.)*

Vivian: Hi, Bink, Hi Bob.

Binky: Vivian.

Vivian: How you doing?

Binky: Not bad.

Mrs. Rudich *(offstage):* Leonard!

Vivian: Hot enough for ya?

Binky: Yes.

Vivian: Sure wish I could go someplace this weekend.

Bob: Me, too. It says here that by the year 2000 we won't have any more travel problems.

Vivian: Really?

Bob: Yes. It says that there'll just be this pill you take.

Vivian: Well, I sure wish we had one now.

Mrs. Rudich *(offstage yell): Leonard!*

Binky: Would you please see what Mom wants, Bob?

Bob: What is it, Mrs. Rudich?

Mrs. Rudich: Lunch time.

Vivian: What do you think, Binky, about those pills?

Binky: It sounds fishy to me.

Vivian: Uh huh.

Bob: It's time for lunch, Bink.

Vivian: It sounds fishy to me, too.

Bob: Your mom says it's time for lunch.

Binky: Tell Mom I'll be right down, would you, Bob?

Vivian: How are *you*, Bobby?

Bob: He'll be right down, Missus R.

Mrs. Rudich: *Thank* you, Bob.

Bob: I'm fine, Viv, thank you.

Vivian: What are you guys working on?

(**Binky** *makes a shhssing sound.*)

Vivian *(to* **Bob***):* What's he working on?

Bob: We've got this clock.

Vivian: Clock, huh?

Bob: Yes.

Vivian: What kind of clock, Bink?

Binky: Two-speed.

Vivian: Two-speed clock, huh?

Binky: Yes.

Vivian: How about that.

Bob: Yes. *(Pause.)*

Vivian: What's it do?

Bob: We don't know.

Mrs. Rudich: *LEONARD!*

Binky: Tell her we'll be right down, will you, Bob?

Bob: Right.

Vivian: Don't get up, Bob, I'll tell her.

(**Vivian** *climbs in through the window and goes to the door.*)

Binky: Thank you, Vivian.

Vivian: He's coming, Missus Rudich.

Mrs. Rudich *(offstage):* Well, tell him to get down here.

Vivian: I will. They'll be right down.

Mrs. Rudich *(offstage):* 'Cause this casserole isn't going to stand around forever.

Vivian: Alright.

Bob: I hate casserole.

Mrs. Rudich: And do you want to stay to lunch?

Vivian: I'd love to, thank you.

Binky: Hand me the pliers, would you, Bob?

Mrs. Rudich *(offstage, to* **Vivian***):* Well, go and call your mother.

Binky *(to* **Bob***):* Thank you.

Vivian *(shouting to* **Mrs. Rudich***):* It's alright, I told her you would ask me.

Mrs. Rudich *(offstage):* Alright, then. *(Pause.)* You tell the two of them to get down here.

Vivian: They're coming.

*(***Binky** *is beginning to become excited while working.* **Bob** *stands next to him and supplies him with the necessary instruments.)*

Vivian: Your mom says to come to lunch, Bink.

Binky: Hammer.

Bob: Right.

Binky: Spoon.

Bob: Gotcha.

Binky: Gimme a bottletop.

Bob: Don't got none.

Binky: Gimme another spoon.

Vivian: I think you're ticking her off.

Bob: Ssshhh!

Binky: A tweezers. (**Binky** *and* **Bob** *busy themselves.*) What time have you got?

Bob: Twelve-eighteen.

Mrs. Rudich *(offstage): LEONARD!!!!*

Binky *(under his breath):* How can you get any work done around here?

Mrs. Rudich *(her voice closer):* Leonard, I'm coming up.

Binky: Hand me those scissors, Bob. *(Pause.)* What's she say?

Bob: She's coming up.

Binky: Lock the door, Bob.

Bob: Right.

(They go back to their business.)

Binky: I think we've just about got it.

Vivian: What?

Binky: Two-speed clock.

Vivian: What's it do?

*(**Mrs. Rudich** is at the door. She tries the door, finds it locked, and pounds on it.)*

Mrs. Rudich: Leonard? Leonard? You come down and eat your meal, do you hear? Vivian?

Bob: Five minutes.

Mrs. Rudich: If you're not down in five minutes, I am going to call your father.

Bob *(under his breath):* He hates casserole.

(Mrs. Rudich retreats.)

Binky: I've got it. Bob, I think that I have got it.

Mrs. Rudich *(offstage):* Do you hear?

(Pause.)

Binky: I lost it.

Bob: The two-speed.

Vivian: Clock.

Binky: Yes. *(Pause.)* I almost had it. *(Pause.)*

Vivian: I'm sorry, Bink.

Binky: I can't get any work done here. I've got to get a place to get away.

Bob: Yes.

Binky: I wish I had a place of my own.

Vivian: You're only twelve, Binky.

Binky: I need a place where I can work. Out in the country just for me and Bob.

Bob *(under his breath):* I need a place, too, Binky.

Binky: You could have your *own* place out there.

Bob: Thank you.

Binky: And a lot of land, and *graze*, and things like that. And eat grass.

Bob: I don't like grass.

Binky: I forgot.

Bob: I'm very fond of human food.

Binky: I know.

Bob: I just hate casserole.

Vivian: I don't blame you.

Binky: And Vivian could visit us.

Vivian: I could?

Binky: Sure.

Vivian: Thanks, Binky.

Binky: Don't thank me, it's only talk at this point.

Vivian: Okay. *(Pause.)*

Binky: I almost had it.

Vivian: What would it have done, Bink?

Binky: My two-speed clock?

Vivian: Yes.

Binky: I'll tell you.

Vivian: Okay.

Binky: I'm not sure . . .

Vivian: Uh huh . . .

Binky: But through our research, Bob and I think that there may just be two kinds of time.

Vivian: Two kinds.

Bob: Yes.

Binky: And we're caught in *one* time, when we get up or we go play ball or visiting, and the time moves at the same speed all the time, but there's another speed.

Bob *(under his breath):* We think.

Binky: Another speed of time.

Bob: That's very slow.

Binky: If we could find it . . .

Bob: . . . everything would stand still.

Binky: . . . on the earth . . .

Bob: . . . and we . . .

Binky: . . . and we would spin off.

Vivian: Where would we spin off to?

Binky: I don't know, Viv.

Bob: To another galaxy?

Binky: Another land, another time.

Bob: Another part of town . . .

Binky: *I* don't know.

Bob: *Any*where.

Binky: There's lots of places in the world, we don't know they *exist* now . . .

Bob: Indiana.

Vivian: Bob, I've heard of Indiana. *(Pause.)*

Bob: Lately?

Vivian: No.

Mrs. Rudich: Leonard, time's up.

Binky: I wish we could go someplace peaceful.

Mrs. Rudich *(again):* Time's up.

Binky: Far from home.

Mrs. Rudich *(irritated):* You come eat lunch right *now*.

Binky: Oh, well.

Bob: We'll do some more after lunch.

Binky: I almost had it.

Vivian: It's okay, Binky.

Mrs. Rudich: Alright, I'm coming up . . .

Binky: I'm not even hungry . . .

Vivian: Don't be depressed, Bink.

Binky: Alright.

Vivian: Even a stopped clock is right once a day.

Binky: Not this one.

Mrs. Rudich: Alright for *you*, Binky Rudich . . .

Binky: Bob, tell Mom we're coming, please.

Bob: Sure. *(He goes to door, opens it and* **Mrs. Rudich** *enters).*

Binky *(to clock):* You — why don't you work!? *(Hits clock with a hammer. There is a bizarre explosion.* **Mrs. Rudich** *freezes while* **Binky, Bob** *and* **Vivian** *start to spin off the earth.)*

Bob: Binky . . .

Binky: What?

Bob: Bink, I think you've got it running right.

Vivian: Binky, I'm scared.

Binky: It's alright, Vivian.

Vivian: What's happening?

Binky: I think we're spinning off the earth.

Bob: About time.

Vivian: Spinning off the earth! Oh, no!

Bob: We're *really* going to miss lunch *now*.

Scene Two

Binky, Bob *and* **Vivian** *are transported to a lonely outpost on Crestview. Two* **Space Pandas** *are changing the guard.*

Panda 1: "Fiat Tibi Quo Pax."

Panda 2: "Eee I Eee I Oh."

(They change the guard, then sit on the floor and proceed to play "Fish," a card game.)

Bob: Where are we?

Vivian: Where are we, Binky?

Binky: Search me.

Vivian: I wonder where we are?

Bob: I'm famished.

(**Binky** *gets up, goes to* **Pandas**.*)*

Binky: Uh . . . Excuse me . . .

Panda 2: What?

Bob: Ask him where a guy could maybe get a bite to eat.

Panda 1: Is that a sheep?

Binky: Yes.

Bob: What's it to ya?

Panda 1: Long time since we saw a sheep here.

Binky: Uh . . .

Panda 1: Only sheep we ever saw here recently was in the movies.

Vivian: Could you please tell us where we are?

Bob: What do you mean "a long time since you saw a sheep"?

Panda 1: Where are you?

Binky: Yes. *(Pause.)*

Panda 1: Crestview. *(Pause.)*

Bob: Where is this place?

Panda 2: What place?

Bob: Crestview.

Panda 2: Right here. I told you.

Panda 1: Last time that we had a sheep here was maybe six, eight thousand years ago.

Panda 2: Where are *you* from?

Vivian: We're all from Waukegan.

Panda 2: Where is that?

Panda 1: A big grey sheep.

Vivian: In Northern Illinois.

Panda 1: Looked just like you.

Vivian: Outside Chicago.

Panda 1: Used to cut that stuff off his back and knit up these stockingcaps out of it.

Panda 2: In Illinois?

Vivian: Yes.

Panda 1: Nifty little things.

Panda 2: What are you doing *here*?

Panda 1: I'm talking, maybe seven thousand years ago . . .

Bob: Where are we?

Panda 2: Crestview. Fourth World in the Goolagong System. The Pearl of the Goose Nebula, the Sweetheart of Space Sector Five. It ain't much, but it's home.

Bob: These guys look just like *pandas*.

Panda 2: How in heck did you get here?

Vivian: How far from Waukegan are we?

Panda 2: Fifty light-years away.

Vivian: How far's that?

Panda 2: What's your name?

Vivian: Vivian.

Panda 2: Vivian what?

Vivian: Mooster.

Panda 2: My name's Boots.

Vivian: Glad to meet you. This is my friend Binky.

Binky: Leonard Rudich.

Panda 2: Hi there.

Binky: Hello.

Panda 2: This is Buffy.

Panda 1: Hi. You're a sheep.

Bob: Yes.

Panda 1: Just *like* a sheep, isn't he?

Bob: My name's Bob.

Panda 1: Pleased to meet you. Glad to have you here. *(Pause.* **Pandas** *go back to their card game.)* Have you got any tens?

Panda 2: Afraid not.

Panda 1: Guess I'm going to fish here, then.

Panda 2: Go to it.

*(***Binky*** *exhibits consternation.)*

Bob: What's up?

Vivian: Binky, what's the matter?

Binky: The clock stopped.

Vivian: What?

Binky: The clock just stopped. *(Pause.)*

Bob: Oh gosh.

Panda 1: Okay, now I'm going to take a shot. Do you have any sevens?

Panda 2: No.

Vivian: The two-speed clock stopped.

Binky: Yes.

Vivian: We're lost then, right? *(Pause.)* Binky, are we lost?

Panda 2: You got a jack?

Vivian: We're lost. We're stranded up in space here, and we'll never get back home again, let alone lunchtime. *(Pause.)* I lied and I didn't tell where I was going. I'll never see Mama again, and I'm real scared.

Binky: Now don't be upset, Vivian. We can work this out.

Vivian: I hope so, Binky. I'm going to catch the dickens if I get home. *(To herself:)* Goin' out in space . . . last year I couldn't cross the *street* alone.

Bob *(to* **Pandas***):* Excuse me?

Panda 1: Yes?

Bob: How far from earth are we?

Panda 1: Fifty light-years.

Vivian: And how far is that?

Binky: A long, long way. Um . . .

Panda 1: Yes?

Binky: We're lost.

Panda 2: You are not lost, you're right on Crestview.

Binky: I know, but we got up here by accident, and now we can't go home.

Panda 1: Why not?

Binky: Our clock stopped.

Panda 2: And you want to get home.

Vivian: Yes.

Panda 1: No problem there.

Binky: No?

Panda 2: No. Of course not. We'll just send you back.

Bob: You will?

Panda 2: Sure.

Vivian: How?

Panda 2: We'll just use the Spatial Relocator. *(Pause.)*

Vivian: You can send us right home?

Panda 2: Sure. *(Pause.)*

Bob: In time for lunch?

Panda 2: They won't know you've been gone. While you're gone, all the time will be froze.

Bob: The time will be froze and they won't know we're gone?

Panda 2: That is right.

Bob: That's *alright* . . .

Vivian: We can go home now?

Panda 2: Hey, stick around a while.

Vivian: We should get back . . .

Panda 2: They won't know that you're gone.

Bob: They won't know that we're gone, Viv.

Vivian: They won't?

Bob: That's what Boots says. We stay here for lunch, and then they shoot us home. The time is froze. We get to eat again.

Vivian: Well . . .

Bob: What do you say, Binky?

Binky: I'll tell you, Bob, it isn't every day a fellow gets a chance to roam around a foreign planet.

Panda 2: Would you like to stay for lunch?

Binky: Viv?

Vivian *(pause):* I guess so.

Panda 1 *(to* **Bob***):* You guys eat grass, huh?

Bob: I have been known to eat a sandwich.

Panda 2: Stay for lunch, we'll give a little tour and you can scoot home when you're ready.

Binky: Okay, Vivian?

Vivian: Okay, Binky.

Binky: Bob?

Bob: Sure, long as I can eat.

Panda 2: Swell.

Bob: Good. Interesting place you've got here.

Panda 1: It's alright. You don't eat grass, huh?

Bob: Not if I can help it.

(They all start to leave for lunch.)

Panda 2 *(to* **Vivian***):* You any relation to the St. Louis Moosters?

Vivian: Not at all.

Panda 1 *(to* **Bob***):* You hungry?

Bob: Starved.

Panda 1: We're having this great casserole today.

Bob: Mmmmm.

*(***Binky** *and* **Vivian** *lag a bit behind.* **Pandas** *and* **Bob** *pull ahead and their conversation fades.)*

Panda 1: You make wool, huh?

Bob: I *can* . . .

Panda 1: Bet you can't do *rayon*, though, huh?

Bob: No.

Panda 1: Mmmm.

*(***Pandas** *and* **Bob** *exit.)*

Vivian: Binky . . .

Binky: Yes, Viv.

Vivian: What do you think?

Binky: It's an adventure, that's for sure.

Vivian: Do you think they'll get us home?

Binky: Well, they said they would.

Vivian: Do you think that the time's really froze while we're gone?

Binky: Well, you saw my mom.

Vivian: If the time froze while we're gone, they won't ever believe us when we get home.

Binky: I know. That's alright, though, huh?

Vivian: I guess so.

Binky: Are you hungry?

Vivian: A little.

Binky: You want to go eat?

Vivian: Okay. *(Pause.)* Binky?

Binky: Yes?

Vivian: Don't Boots and Buffy look like pandas?

Binky: They sure do.

Vivian: I thought so . . .

(Binky and Vivian exit and walk into lunch.)

Scene Three

At rise: The dining room of Crestview. **Binky, Bob, Vivian** *and the* **Pandas** *are eating lunch. The dining room is crowded with various "Crestviewian" types. There is a hubbub.*

Buffy: Don't get food like this back in Waukegan, huh, Bob?

Bob: Ummmm.

Boots *(to* **Binky***):* So you're an inventor.

Binky: Yes.

Boots *(to* **Vivian***):* And what do you do, Vivian?

Vivian: I, you know, I go to school and stuff.

Boots: Uh huh.

Buffy: They whip it up from these huge jobs that they get on the moon.

Bob: Delicious.

Buffy: They call it Lunafish.

Bob *(under his breath): Tastes* like it.

Vivian: I also play the piccolo.

Boots: Uh huh. And what do you want to be when you grow up . . . you're a child, right?

Vivian: I'm a young woman.

Boots: Uh huh.

Vivian: When I grow up all I want to be is flexible.

Boots: Ummm.

Buffy: Good for ya, too!

Vivian: My mom says best thing you can be is flexible when you grow up.

Boots: I totally agree.

Vivian: I kinda miss her.

Boots: Miss your mom?

Vivian: Yes.

Boots: Well, we'll send you right back after lunch.

Vivian: You're sure?

Boots: Sure.

Bob: Why'd they name this planet Crestview?

Buffy: Thought it might attract investors.

Bob: Oh.

Binky: Nice place you've got here.

Boots: Thank you.

(Suddenly there are sounds of trumpets and cymbals.)

Offstage Voice: Make way for His Magnificence, His Highness, His Omnipotent Persuasive Powers, The Star of the Six Satellites, the Scourge of the Goose Nebula. *(Sounds of honking.)* Knock that off . . . *(All bow down to the ground, save our three earthlings.)*

George *(to a* **Retainer***):* They aren't bowing down.

Retainer: They're new here.

George: Bow them down.

Retainer *(to* **Binky,** **Bob** *and* **Vivian***):* Bow down. *(They bow down.)* His Bite is Merciless, His Bark is Worse, The Greatest Thing since Sliced Bread: here he is: GEORGE TOPAX!

(All, except **Binky,** **Bob** *and* **Vivian,** *chant: "Hail to thee, oh Topax.")*

Bob *(quietly to* **Binky***):* What's his name?

Binky: I didn't catch it.

Bob *(to* **Boots***):* What's this guy called?

Retainer: Silence! Silence during the ceremony. Who was talking? *(Pause.)* We're going to stay here until who was talking 'fesses up. *(Pause.)* I can wait. *(Pause.)* I'd hate to punish the whole lot of you.

Vivian *(under her breath):* Oh, oh . . .

George: You can't get respect around here any more.

Retainer: You'd better just admit it.

George *(beckons* **Retainer***, softly):* Whack 'em on the head with a pumpkin.

Retainer: Unless whoever's talking 'fesses up right now, we're going to whack each individual right on top of the head with a big pumpkin. *(Pause. To* **Offstage Assistant***:)* Bring in the pumpkin. (**Assistant** *brings in a huge pumpkin.*) I don't want to have to do this.

Bob: I'm not going to like this, Bink.

Retainer: Okay. Everybody line up. Anybody who flinches gets another one for flinching.

Bob: I don't want to see everybody get whacked on the head.

Vivian: No.

(Everybody in the cafeteria gets reluctantly into line. The **Retainer** *gets ready to whack the first individual out.)*

George *(under his breath):* And don't think I enjoy this.

Retainer: And don't think he enjoys this!

(There are drumrolls, cymbals clashing, etc. **George** *looks away and puts his fingers in his ears.)*

Retainer *(to* **Assistant***):* Do it.

Bob: Wait!

(All stop and look at **Bob***, who steps out of line.)*

Retainer: What?

Bob: *I* was talking.

Retainer: You were?

Bob: Yes. *(Pause.)*

Retainer: Everybody sit down. *(They do so.)* So what'd you want to do a thing like that for? How long have you been here, anyway?

Bob: About a half an hour.

Retainer: Yeah? *(Pause.)*

Bob: We came from earth.

Retainer: From earth?

Bob: Yes.

Retainer *(aside):* How about that? *(Pokes* **George***.)* Sire.

Bob *(to* **Binky***): What's* his name? *(***Binky** *shrugs.)*

Retainer: Sire . . .

George: You do it yet?

Retainer: No, Sire . . . *(Takes fingers out of* **George's** *ears.)*

George: What?

Retainer: These people say they came from . . . where?

Binky: We're from Waukegan.

George: That is no excuse.

Binky: We only got here.

George: That is no excuse at all. If you can't take a joke, why, just stay home, then. *(To* **Retainer***:)* Whack 'em out, the both of 'em.

Vivian: Binky . . .

George: Who said Binky?

Retainer: Who said Binky?

Vivian: *I* did.

George: Who's that?

Bob: Vivian.

George: She a friend of yours?

Binky: Yes.

George: Whack her out, too, for good measure.

Retainer: Get up here.

*(***Vivian** *goes and stands next to them.* **George** *is still looking away.)*

George: Okay, let's just do this and we'll get it over with. I'm starving. What's for lunch?

Retainer *(announcing):* What is for lunch?

Offstage Voice: Lunafish.

George: Casserole?

Retainer *(to* **Offstage Voice***):* Casserole?

Offstage Voice: Yes. *(Pause.)*

George *(to* **Retainer***):* Send out for a sandwich.

Bob: I feel the same way.

George: Whack 'em out.

(There is a drumroll. The three are walked to a huge contraption over which is suspended a monstrous pumpkin. They wave goodbye to **Buffy** *and* **Boots** *and embrace each other.)*

Retainer: On the count of three. *(To* **Executioner***:)* ONE!

Executioner: I'm not ready yet.

Retainer: Well, tell me when you're ready.

George: What?

Retainer: He isn't set up.

*(***George*** snorts.)*

Executioner: I'm ready.

Retainer: Alright. ONE!

Executioner: We *did* one!

Retainer: You weren't ready so we're doing one again. Okay?

Executioner: Okay.

Retainer: You ready?

Executioner: Yes.

Retainer: Alright. ONE!

Vivian: Goodbye, Bink.

Binky: Goodbye, Vivian.

Vivian: Bob.

Bob: Vivian, goodbye.

Retainer: TWO!

Vivian: Goodbye, Bob.

Bob: Goodbye, Bink.

Binky: So long, Bob.

Retainer: READY, GET SET . . .

Bob: If I have only one life to lead, let me lead it as a sheep.

George: *STOP THE EXECUTION!*

Retainer: *STOP THE EXECUTION!*

George: A sheep? *(He turns around and sees* **Bob** *for the first time.)* That man's a sheep! Turn him loose, turn them *all* loose. My friends, come up here . . . *(To* **Executioner***:)* Turn 'em *loose* . . .

Executioner *(to* **Binky, Bob** *and* **Vivian***):* G'wan, get.

George: Come up here, come up here.

Retainer: Give 'em room, give 'em room.

(The three dazed earthlings wander up to the podium. On the way up **Bob** *passes by* **Buffy***.)*

Bob *(quietly, in passing):* What's this guy's name?

Retainer: Silence!

George: It's alright. Come up, come up, my friends. *(They start to go towards him.)* Yeeeessss! Come right up to Topax.

Vivian: Hi.

George: Hel*lo!* Now you're from *where?*

Binky: From earth.

George: From *earth.* How *won*derful for you. What part?

Binky: Waukegan.

George *(with great feeling):* Waukegan.

Bob: You been there?

George: No. I can't say that I have. Wau-ke-gan . . . *(Pause.)* It sure is fun to say, though. Wau*ke*gan.

Bob: Mmmm.

George: Let's everybody say it. *(Pause.)*

Retainer: Everybody Say Waukegan! *(Beat.)*

All *(listlessly):* Waukegan.

George: You said it. *(To* **Retainer***:)* Make 'em feel at home.

Retainer: Mmmm. *(Pause.)*

George: Yep, yep, yep. Say, sorry about almost dropping that huge pumpkin on your heads, eh?

Binky: Not at all.

Vivian: A good thing that you stopped.

George: It sure is.

Vivian: We'd of all been covered with some orange glop.

George: Yes, you would. You would have.

Bob: Yes. *(Pause.)*

George: So! So you came up here, eh?

Vivian: We got spun right off the earth.

George: Well, how about that? How'd you manage that?

Bob: How do you think?

George: A two-speed clock? *(They nod.)* Well. Well, anything that I can do to make your stay more pleasant, you just tell me. Will you do that?

Bob: Sure thing.

George: Don't be shy now . . .

Vivian: No. We wouldn't.

George: Anything you'd like to *see* . . . or anything . . . or *eat* . . . *(To* **Retainer:***)* They eat lunch?

Retainer: You bet you, Sire.

George: Good. Real good. Uh huh . . . the sights, or anything, you name it.

Vivian: Actually, we just were going home.

George: You're going where?

Bob *(pausing):* Home.

George: Home.

Vivian: Yes. *(Pause.)*

George: Whatever *for*? *(Pause.)*

Vivian: We live there.

George: Oh.

Vivian: Our friends said they were going to shoot us back to, you know, back to earth when we were finished lunch.

George: They did?

Vivian: Yes.

George: Who, who told you that?

Vivian: Those guys, they looked a little bit like . . . *(Pause.)*

George: Like what?

Vivian: Like, you know, like these pandas.

George: Told you they would send you back to earth.

Vivian: Yes.

George: And, of course, we will.

Vivian: You will?

George: Most certainly.

Vivian: When?

George: Anytime you want. *(Pause.)*

Bob: Now.

George: Now? Absolutely. Just as soon as we have made arrangements to prepare the . . . *(To* **Retainer***) . . .* Whatda we call that thing?

Retainer: That space-shooter thing?

George: Yeah.

Retainer: Uh, . . . the . . . I knew it this morning . . . *(Generally:)* What do we call that job that shoots things through space very quickly?

Citizen: A palatial something.

Retainer: Spatial Relocator. *(To* **George:***)* A Spatial Relocator, Topax.

George: *I* knew that . . . We'll put you in the, uh, wha-chacallit and we'll shoot you back. We'll shoot you right back home. *(To* **Retainer***:)* Get that thing revved up.

Retainer: You bet. *(He exits.)*

George: And while we're revving up, perhaps you'd like to see a bit of Crestview, eh, what do you say?

Binky: Well . . .

George: While we're getting that job all prepared and so on. It's not every day you get a chance to tour a foreign planet fifty light-years from your home.

Vivian: That's true.

George: We're really very proud of it up here.

Vivian: It's lovely.

George: I'll go set it up, you'll walk around, you'll take a little tour. We'll get you home in time for anthracite.

Binky: For what?

George: For anthracite. *(Pause.)* Whatever it is that you eat when the sun goes down.

Vivian: Dinner?

Bob: It's his planet, he can call it what he wants.

Binky: You're right. Well, thank you very much . . . *(To* **Bob***:) What's* his name? *(***Bob** *shrugs.)* Thank you very much, Your Mmmglmmmf.

George: Pleasure.

Binky: We'd be glad to take a little tour around.

George: Never regret it. *(***Retainer** *returns and* **George**

calls to him.) Hank, Hank, I'd like to . . . **(George** *moves toward* **Hank** *and passes out of earshot of the three earthlings.* **Hank's** *and* **George's** *dialogue gets mumbled and comes up after the following:)*

Vivian: Something's fishy, Bink.

Binky: I know it.

Bob: Lunafish.

Vivian: No, something else.

Binky: She's right.

Bob: What is it?

Binky: I don't know, but I think that we're going to find out.

Bob: I kind of think so, too, Binky.

Vivian: Yeah.

Bob: I'm glad they're gonna send us home soon.

Vivian: So am I.

George *(to* **Retainer***):* That sheep is not to leave the planet.

Retainer: Yes, Your Topax.

George: I *am* Topax.

Retainer: Yes, you are.

George: The other two may go, but he stays.

Retainer: Yes.

George: Or *everyone* gets whacked upon the head.

Retainer: Your wish is our command.

George: I know it. See that they do not suspect a thing.

Retainer: I will.

George: Repeat what I said back to me.

Retainer: "What I said back to me."

George: Before that.

Retainer: The boy and girl may go, the sheep must stay.

George: Thus runs the world away.

Retainer: I've got it.

George: Good.

(George *and* **Retainer** *wander back towards the three earthlings. Both groups behave nonchalantly.)*

George: And make sure that they see the new car wash.

Retainer: I shall.

Bob: And some *sights*. We'd love to see some sights.

Retainer: We've got 'em.

George: Yes sirree, we got 'em here. You're looking to see sights, just come to Crestview.

Vivian: That's swell.

Binky: Yes, it is.

George: Yep, yep, yep, yep.

Bob: Uh huh.

Retainer: You *bet* you.

George: Well, we better, yeah, we better go and start the tour, huh, what say?

Binky: Fine with me. With you, Vivian?

Vivian: Absolutely.

George: Fine, then.

Binky: Bob?

Bob: What?

Binky: Start the tour up?

Bob: Well, certainez-moi.

Retainer: You bet.

George: Here we go, then.

Retainer: Yup, yup, yup.

Binky: Here we go.

(**Bob** *starts to go.*)

George: Half-a-dollar tour of Crestview, starting now.

Retainer: A-one, a two, a three . . .

(*They all stand there.*)

George (*suddenly*): *Seize the sheep!*

Bob: What he say?

(**Retainer** *and others attempt to seize* **Bob, the sheep.**)

Vivian: Bink, they're trying to get Bob!

Binky: Run, Bob, *run* . . .

George (*shouting*): Grab him, snatch him . . .

(**Vivian** *defends* **Bob's** *rear through karate as the escape is attempted.*)

Bob: Come on, Viv.

Binky: Come on!!

(The three make good their escape, thrusting themselves into the unknown of darkest Crestview.)

George: We lost them?

Retainer: She's real tough, chief.

George: Bring them back. I want them back within the hour. Bring the sheep to me; the girl and boy, I want them whacked out with the largest pumpkin 'ere a man can find. Go, get out of here. *(Pause.)* I'm very disappointed in you.

*(**Retainer** schlumps out of the royal presence. A **Court Jester** appears, singing impromptu ballads of the sorrow of **Topax**.)*

Court Jester:

It looked extremely Rocky for the Crestview boys
    that day,
The Two Kids and the Sheep had gone and stolen
    right away.

George *(to **Citizen**):* Who is that idiot?

Citizen: The new court jester.

Court Jester:

So when Topax said to all his clan,
"Go Find them and Go . . . "

Citizen: Hey . . . *(Pause.)*

Court Jester:

"So when Topax said to all his clan,
Go Find them . . . "

Citizen: Hey! *(Pause.)*

Court Jester: What?

Citizen *(points toward* **Topax***):* Wants to see you.

Court Jester: He wants to see *me*?

*(***Citizen** *nods. Approaches* **Topax** *and bows.)*

George: Get up. *(***Citizen** *does so.)* Where do you get off singing that drivel?

Court Jester: It's Art, Sire. *(Long pause.)*

George: Geddouddahere.

*(***Court Jester** *exits.* **George** *sits. He spies two-speed clock and goes to it.)*

George *(generally):* Somebody lose this?

Scene Four

Binky, **Bob** *and* **Vivian** *are on the run from the forces of* **Topax**. **Binky** *is figuring on a pad.*

Bob: What do you think they want with *me*?

Binky: Beats me, Bob.

Bob: Viv?

Vivian: I couldn't tell you.

Binky: I think that I've got it.

Vivian: What?

Binky: I think I've figured out how come the clock stopped.

Vivian: You did?

Binky: Well, I think I did. I think if I could get a bobbypin . . .

Offstage Voice: Now hear this: The two earthlings, Binky Rudich and Vivian Rooster . . .

Vivian: Mooster. *(Her two companions fall on her to silence her.)*

Offstage Voice: And their companion, Bob, the Sheep, have *(pause)* . . . Correction, that should be Vivian *Moo*ster . . .

Vivian: Thank you.

Offstage Voice: Have escaped. George Topax wants those earthlings. Bad. And he has issued a reward of fifty-thousand Kapoks . . .

Bob: I wonder how much a Kapok is?

Offstage Voice: One Kapok being equal to approximately three of the earthling bucks . . .

Bob: That's a lot of moola!

Offstage Voice: For the arrest of the earthlings and the sheep, be on the lookout. The earthling Boy and Girl are of Small to Medium height, the Mooster Person has her hair in Braids and the picture of some kind of animal on her T-Shirt.

Vivian: It's a mouse.

Offstage Voice: The Rudich individual has on a stained, gray laboratory smock. He has a stethoscope around his neck and wears a Chicago White Sox baseball cap.

Binky: They're very observant.

Offstage Voice: Baseball is a sport on earth. The White Sox have not had a team worth mentioning since 1959.

Vivian: He's right *there*.

Bob: *That's* for sure.

Offstage Voice: The group's third member is a sheep.

Bob: Yup.

Offstage Voice: He is large and white and needs a bath.

(**Binky** *and* **Vivian** *endeavor to hide* **Bob** *as best they can.*)

Offstage Voice: Great care should be exercised in attempting this sheep's capture. Topax wants this animal in one piece. If you break it, you've bought it, dig it? If you've got the Beat, go get the Sheep. Once again, whoever finds the earthlings gets the Kapoks. If they aren't found by tomorrow night, nobody gets to go to the movies.

Vivian: We gotta get out of here.

Offstage Voice: And tomorrow night's movie is "Penguins on Parade."

(*Assorted catcalls.*)

Offstage Voice: The *original* version with Lola Laguna and Edward Farpis.

Binky: You know, I'd like to see that.

Offstage Voice: So go out and get hot, turkeys. (*Pause.*) That is all. (*Pause.*)

Bob: We gotta get *outta* here.

Vivian: Any ideas, Bink?

Binky: Well, I'll tell you, Vivian, the way I see it, what we have to do is get our hands back on the two-speed clock.

Bob: Now, that's for sure. We got to get the two-speed clock to Bink, you get my boy a bobbypin, and he'll have us in Waukegan in no time flat. Huh, Bink?

Binky: Well, Bob, the first thing we must do is get inside the Palace.

Vivian: Yes.

Binky: And they'll be on the lookout for us.

Bob: You can bet your last Kapok on that, Bink.

Binky: So I think that what we have to do is wait for night, and figure out some way to sneak in there.

Bob: Right.

(Two of Crestview's finest, the **Space Pandas**, *walk past.)*

Panda 1: I've always wanted to see "Penguins on Parade."

Panda 2: I saw the remake.

Panda 1: Yes? How was it?

Panda 2: Not too good.

Panda 1: No, huh?

Panda 2: No.

Panda 1: Hmm. That Lola Laguna, she could act, though.

Panda 2: And how about Edward Farpis, huh? Couldn't he act?

Panda 1: He could act.

Panda 2: You're darn right he could. *(Pause.)*

Panda 1: Say, whatever happened to him?

Panda 2: Edward Farpis?

Panda 1: Yeah.

Panda 2: Disappeared. No one knows.

Panda 1: Well, I'd sure like to go to those movies.

Panda 2: I could use them fifty-thousand Kapoks.

Panda 1: You take over there, and I'll take over here.

*(The **Pandas** split up and begin their search.)*

Bob: I sure wish we were back in Waukegan.

Vivian: Let's get outta here . . .

*(The three sneak off; as they do so, **Binky** loses his White Sox hat and has to go back for it. As he goes back for it, one of the **Pandas** sits on the stoop right in front of him.)*

Panda 1: That you, Boots?

Binky: Mmm.

Panda 1: Yeah, if I had those Kapoks, you know what I'd do?

Binky: Nnnn.

Panda 1: I'd buy me a van, and I'd get it fit out with a stereo.

Binky: Mmmm.

Panda 1: And I'd drive it all over.

Binky: *Mmmm.*

Panda 1: What would you do if it's you got the money? *(He turns around and sees **Binky**. Pause.)*

Binky: Hi there.

Panda 1: Hi.

Binky: You're looking for the earthlings, I bet.

Panda 1: Yup.

Binky: Yeah. Me, too. I figured the best way to catch them was to dress up like them so that I could infiltrate their organization.

Panda 1: Uh huh.

Binky: Had a heck of a time finding this White Sox cap.

Panda 1: Mmmm.

Binky: Yep, yep. *(Pause.)* Well, good luck. I'll be seeing ya.

Panda 1 *(detaining* **Binky***):* In the name of the Five Asteroids, and the Six Suns of Sauganash, and through the power vested in me by his Great Serenity, George Topax, I now pronounce you man and wife. *(Pause.)*

Binky: I beg your pardon?

Panda 1: I'm sorry. I mean, you're under arrest.

(The **Panda** *walks* **Binky** *off.* **Vivian** *and* **Bob** *come back looking for him.)*

Vivian: Bink?

Bob: Binky?

Vivian: Bink?

Bob: Where'd you go to?

Offstage Voice: Now get this. The earthling Rudich has been apprehended.

Bob: They caught him?

Offstage Voice: Unless the sheep Bob and Ms. Vivian
. . . *(aside)* . . . what's her name? *(Pause.)* Mooster . . .

Vivian: *Thank* you.

Offstage Voice: Present themselves right away at the
great throne of Topax, Rudich will have a big pumpkin
dropped on his head. *(Pause.)* Think it over, you've got
half an hour.

Vivian: Oh, gosh.

Offstage Voice: P.S. "Penguins on Parade," the original
version with Lola Laguna and Edward Farpis *will* be
shown tomorrow night, weather permitting. That's it.

Bob: Half an hour.

Vivian: Oh, gosh.

Bob: Well, we've got to go give ourselves up.

Vivian: Let me think for a minute.

Bob: We can't let them go whack out Bink.

Vivian: But we can't give you up, either, Bob.

Bob: Yeah.

Vivian: Okay. Let's not get panicky. I'm going to figure this out.

Bob: I'm scared.

Vivian: Don't get scared, Bob, there must be a way out
of this.

Offstage Voice: You've got twenty-five minutes.

Bob: We're *thinking*, we're *thinking*. For pete's sake, just
give us a minute, huh? *(Pause.)* You got any ideas, Viv?

Vivian (*shaking her head*): No.

Bob: Oh, gosh. I sure wish we'd stayed home.

Scene Five

A **T.V. Newsperson** *takes the stage.*

Newsperson: Yes, folks, it's an exciting day up here on scenic Crestview. Started off, here come these three jobs up from earth, turns out that one of 'em's a girl, other one's a boy, and, here's the capper, the third one is a sheep. That's right, you heard me right, a big grey dirty dyed-in-the-wool sheep. Well, when George Topax (may his line continue and improve) saw that sheep, why you can all imagine that all Holy-you-know-what broke loose up here. Now, as most of you know, the three earth-types misused the hospitality of his Infernal Precocity and ran away. (**Binky** *is being held captive by a* **Space Panda** *in back of the* **Newsperson**.) Fine investigative policework on the part of our Space Pandas traced one of the earthlings to his hiding spot. (*Points to* **Binky** *and the* **Panda**.) That's them, the earth-boy and our own Donald "Buffy" Watschalk, the apprehender of the earthling. (**Space Panda** *bows.*) Watschalk, as you know, will receive the reward of fifty-thousand Kapoks and the profound thanks of all us Crestviewians for getting George (Eternal Mercy) Topax to allow us to see "Penguins on Parade" with Edward Farpis and Lola Laguna tomorrow night. Come up here, Donald. (**Panda** *does so.*) I'd like to thank you on behalf of all of us.

Panda 1: It's just my duty, Bill.

Newsperson: I think it's something more than that. It took a lot of guts and savvy to bring that boy in.

Panda 1: No, Bill, anybody on the Pandas would of done the same. I just got lucky.

Newsperson: Do you hear that, Folks? He just got lucky. Well, we think that it was something more than that. What are you going to do with all those Kapoks, Don?

Panda 1: Bill, I thought I'd spend them.

Newsperson: On what?

Panda 1: Things.

Newsperson: You heard it here first, folks, he'd spend the Kapoks on some "things." Don "Buffy" Watschalk of the Space Pandas. And now we're going to have a word with the young boy that all this is about, the escaped earthling this man apprehended, Binky Radish.

Binky: Rudich.

Newsperson: Now, Binky, you're from where?

Binky: Waukegan, earth.

Newsperson: Well, you're a long way from Waukegan, that's for sure. What made you come up here to Crestview?

Binky: I am a scientist. I came because it was here.

Newsperson: Uh huh. Would you have come here had it *not* been here?

Binky: No.

Newsperson: Where would you have gone in that case?

Binky: Somewhere else.

Newsperson: You heard it here first, he would have gone some *other* place. And how about that superb job of police work that this panda did in apprehending you, eh, Binky?

Binky: Ummm.

Newsperson: Yes, folks, his companions are at large. Don, could you give us an estimate of when you foresee capture of the sheep and that Ms. Rooster?

Binky: Mooster.

Panda 1: We're gonna catch 'em any moment.

Binky: Can I ask a question?

Newsperson: I suppose so.

Binky: What does George Topax want with Bob, the sheep?

Newsperson: That's a *good* question.

Binky: Thank you.

Newsperson: Panda Watschalk . . .

Panda 1: Yessir?

Newsperson: Perhaps you would like to tell the earthling and refresh our viewers' memories as to why his Righteous Indignation wants a sheep.

Panda 1: My pleasure. Well, Binky, as you know, our Mighty Topax wants a sheep for wool.

Newsperson: That's right, wool, the thing that sheeps make with their mouths or something.

Binky: It grows on their back.

Newsperson: A little joker! . . . Go on, Don.

Panda 1: He saw this thing, a movie that had . . . *(To*

Binky:) What's that thing with "downs" and "hiking"?

Binky: Football.

Panda 1: Football in it and this one guy had a great big sweater with a letter "N" on it. And he found out that they make them from those sheep jobs.

Binky: Ah. *(Pause.)* He wants a sweater.

Panda 1: Yes. That is correct.

Binky: You don't have wool up here.

Panda 1: You've got the only sheep.

Binky: Couldn't he make one of orlon or dacron or somethin'? Do you have those things up here?

Panda 1: He's allergic.

Binky: Oh. Sorry.

Panda 1: He wants a sweater. He can't wear it unless it's made out of wool and that's why he wants the sheep.

Newsperson: It would be a grand old day for Crestview if George Topax got the sheep, and if he *doesn't* get it, well, folks, we can guess that he is going to ring down the very thunder from the sky, eh, Watschalk?

Panda 1: That's right, Bill.

Newsperson: And I understand that if the sheep does not surrender in about twelve minutes, Binky Rudich here is going to get a great big pumpkin dropped on him.

Panda 1: That's right.

Newsperson: Well, that's the way it goes, and we've been talking to you on remote from right here at the Holy Throne of Topax with Space Panda Donald Watschalk, apprehender of the earthling, and his young apprehendee from Waukegan, Binky Rudich.

Binky: Hi.

Newsperson: This has been Bill Kabirdie, Crestview News Control. And now: back to the story.

Scene Six

Bob *and* **Vivian** *are pacing up and down in an alley.*

Vivian: They're going to drop a pumpkin on his head.

Bob: I know it.

Vivian: We have got to get him out of there.

Bob: I know.

Vivian: If we had gone downstairs to lunch when Mrs. Rudich called us we would not have gotten in this mess.

Bob: You live and learn.

Vivian: What are we going to do?

Bob: Viv, I have no idea.

(Enter a **Derelict.***)*

Derelict: Can you spare a Kapok?

Bob: Uh, no, we're just walking around here. We don't come from, you know, earth, or anything, we just — uh, actually, I grew up not too far from there myself, uh huh. You're probably asking yourself why that fellow is dressed like a sheep. I'll tell you . . .

Vivian: He grew up right near here, right on Crestview.

Bob: Yes. This, when I got up my wife told me that I always wear the same things to the office every day and she was getting tired looking at me all the time in Glen Plaid, and why didn't I put on a sheep suit and be daring for a change.

Vivian: That's right.

Bob: And son-of-a-gun if that drat sheep from earth did not show up and everybody's looking for him.

Vivian: That's the truth.

Bob: So I was going home to change. *(They start to exit.)*

Vivian: Bye.

Derelict: Wait! *(They wait.)*

Bob: Yes?

Derelict: You two are the earthlings!

Bob: No, it's funny you should think that but, in fact . . .

Vivian: . . . uh huh . . .

Bob: In fact . . .

Vivian: . . . yup . . .

Bob *(pause):* Uh . . .

Derelict: You've got fifty-thousand Kapoks on your head! *(Pause.)* That's a lot of moola. *(Pause.)* I haven't had a bite in *days* . . . The last thing that I ate was Luna Casserole.

Bob: I sympathize.

Derelict: If I turn you two in I will be rich!

Bob: Don't turn us in.

Derelict: I will be rich again.

Vivian: Again?

Derelict: You bet you. You may not think it to look at me but I was once the Toast of the Goose Nebula.

Bob: Wouldn't doubt it for a minute.

Derelict: Go ahead and scoff.

Vivian: We aren't scoffing.

Derelict: Everybody else does. What's the use. The world is what it is. *(Pause.)* You got a Kapok for an old guy? *(Pause.)*

Vivian: You aren't going to turn us in?

Derelict: I have been rich and famous. I am scorned and ancient now. I will not spit upon the memory of former triumph and success to turn informer for a sum I would once have considered trivial.

Vivian: You aren't going to turn us in?

Derelict: Go. Go your way. Perhaps you could just lay two or three Kapoks on me for my supper.

Bob: Uh, well, you see, we haven't got a Kapok.

Derelict: You haven't?

Bob: No.

Derelict: What *have* you got?

Vivian: I've got a quarter.

Derelict: What's a quarter?

Vivian: It's a coin from earth.

Derelict: No good. Oh, what's the use.

Bob: What were you rich at?

Derelict: You would not believe me.

Bob: All the things we've seen since we left Binky's attic in Waukegan, I'd believe just about anything.

Derelict: I was once an actor.

Vivian: No!

Derelict: Yes.

Vivian: What were you in?

Derelict: Oh . . . "Hamster in Heaven," "The Revenge of the Space Pandas," "Beast of the Goolagong," "Penguins on Parade," "The Night the . . ."

Vivian: You must be Edward Farpis.

Derelict *(to himself):* They've heard of me.

Bob: Sir, is that who you are?

Derelict: They've heard of me. They've heard of Edward Farpis in Waukegan . . . Yes. I am Farpis.

Bob: How about that? Stuck in an alley with Edward Farpis.

Vivian: How come you don't make films any more?

Derelict: I was a matinee idol and I have grown old. I am no longer useful.

Bob: I'm sorry.

Offstage Voice: You've got five-and-a-half minutes to surrender, sheep, or Rudich gets a Jack-O-Lantern helmet.

Derelict: They are going to drop a pumpkin on his head.

Bob: That's right.

Derelict: George Topax is not a very nice man.

Vivian: No.

Derelict: He'd do anything to get his letter sweater.

Vivian: What are we going to do, Bob?

Derelict: We must get your friend out.

Bob: But the question is how?

Derelict: We have to think.

(They huddle together. **Panda** *walks by.)*

Panda: Hey there. Any of you seen a big, grey, uh, sheep-like affair from earth and a young person who calls herself "Vivian"?

Vivian: No.

Panda: I don't like to put you out, but you look like the two of 'em.

Vivian: How *about* that.

Panda: Think that I am going to have to run you in.

Vivian: Wait. He can vouch for us. *(Indicating* **Derelict.***)*

Panda: He can?

Bob: Bet your booties. He's known us since we were babes.

Panda *(pause. To* **Derelict***):* Well?

Derelict: They're from earth. This is them. Glory be that you came along. They have been holding me hostage.

Panda: Who are you?

Derelict: A bum.

Panda: Well, it's all over now, Old Timer. Yes, Sirree. Now, you two come along and come quietly.

Derelict: That'll teach you with your filthy earth ways and all.

(*The* **Panda** *takes the two off.* **Farpis** *rants after them.*)

Vivian: This is very disappointing, Bob.

Bob: Go understand actors, huh?

Vivian: I guess so.

Scene Seven

The Throne of Topax. **Binky** *is surrounded by* **Pandas.** **George Topax** *is on the throne. The* **Executioner** *is working out with his pumpkins.*

George: How's it working?

Executioner: A-Okay.

George: Good.

Offstage Voice: You've got two minutes to show up, sheep.

George (*pause*): Hey, look, cheer up, these things they happen.

Binky: Thank you.

George: There's no need to take that tone, it's nothing personal.

Executioner *(to* **Binky***):* You mind just standing under here a minute?

Binky: Sure. *(He stands under the pumpkin apparatus. The* **Executioner** *makes adjustments.)* What about Bob and Vivian?

George: Hmmm. What about them?

Binky: When you whack me out they'll be here all alone.

(Throughout this section, the **Executioner** *is heard muttering "One, two, three" and testing the apparatus.)*

George: Uh huh.

Binky: How will they get back to Waukegan?

George: Well, you know, that sheep of yours, at such time as we catch him, isn't going anywhere. Eh? We are going to make a sweater for me out of him.

Binky: And then what?

George: Whack him out.

Executioner: I've never dropped a pumpkin on an animal before.

Binky *(to* **George***):* Why?

George: Why? I will tell you. George Topax gets his sweater.

All: All Hail Topax!

George: Thank you. Then we whack the sheep out, and noooooobody else, huh? in the Whole Great Grey Goose Nebula can have a sweater. I'm the only one.

Binky: Why don't you just send Vivian and Bob back to Waukegan.

George: How?

Binky: What?

George: How'm I gonna do that?

Binky: With the Spatial Relocator.

George: Hey, that hasn't worked in years.

Binky: Oh.

Offstage Voice: One minute.

Binky: Wait. Wait. Let me try to get my two-speed clock to work. Give me a bobbypin.

George: No time.

Binky: But wait. How will Vivian get back?

George: She stays.

Binky: But she's already overdue on her last science project.

George: Tough.

Binky: She'll never graduate. (**Topax** *shrugs.*) This guy is *mean* . . .

Executioner: Heck yes.

George (*to* **Executioner**)*:* You ready?

Executioner: Bet your flaky piecrust, Sire.

George: Go whack him out.

*A processional has begun, leading **Binky** around the Throne Room in a ceremonial fashion, and eventually ending back at the pumpkin guillotine. The **Jester** takes stage.)*

Jester:

Oh, they'd taken Binky Rudich and they'd
Put him on the stand.

And now, they're going to whack him
And no one can lend a hand.
Oh, the hearts of Crestview tremble
At the sight of the brave boy,
Who has grown up in Waukegan and . . .

George: Will somebody get that wimp out of here?

(The **Jester** *is removed. The processional proceeds, and concludes at the pumpkin guillotine.)*

Offstage Voice: That's it, there ain't no more, the time is up.

George: Any last words?

Binky: Why don't you let me try to fix the two-speed clock in case you change your mind?

George: Forget it. *(To* **Executioner***:)* Do it. *(There is a drumroll, suspense, etc.)*

Executioner: ONE! . . . TWO! . . . *(He inhales.)*

(The **Panda** *arrives on the scene with* **Vivian** *and* **Bob***.)*

Panda: Oh, mighty Topax!

Bob *(under his breath):* What's his name?

George: Wait! *(The* **Executioner** *waits.)*

Executioner: Shoot!

Vivian: Binky!

Binky: Vivian! Bob!

George: Got the sheep, huh?

Panda: Yes, Sire.

George: Good work, man. How does it feel *now*, wool-face!

Bob: No comment.

George: Yeah, I hope not . . . leading us a merry chase all over this whole godforsaken planet.

Vivian: At least we've saved our Binky.

George: Saved your Binky, huh?

Vivian: From your dropping the pumpkin on his head.

George: And just how is that, Foster?

Vivian: Mooster. And it's *Ms*. Mooster to you, if you please. *(***George*** snorts.)* And let Binky go, now, we're here.

George: But you didn't give uuppp!

Vivian: So what?

George: So I told you that I would let Binky go if you gave up and you made us go out and catch you, so all bets are off.

Bob: You mean you won't let Binky go?

George: That is what I mean.

Vivian: Binky.

George: Go put the Mooster person in the Concentration Booth with Rudich.

Bob: No! *(Lunges at* **George***.)*

Retainer: Restrain that sheep!

(Various **Space Pandas** *fall on him.* **Vivian** *is taken and put in the execution booth with* **Binky***.)*

Vivian *(to* **Executioner***)*: Why do they call this the Concentration Booth?

Executioner: Because when it's over there's a large concentration of pumpkin all over.

Vivian: That's *sick* . . .

George: Whack 'em out.

Executioner: With pleasure. (*He starts making arrangements.*)

Vivian: Binky . . .

Binky: I know.

Vivian: I never got my science paper done.

Binky: Don't worry, Vivian, it's too late now.

Vivian: Your mom is going to miss you.

Binky: Yup.

Vivian: Goodbye, Bob!

Executioner: One!

Bob: I'll see they pay for this, Viv . . . Bink!

George: Big talk for a sheep.

Binky: Goodbye, Bob.

Executioner: Two!

George: They get a little lanolin, they think they own the world.

(**Binky** *and* **Vivian** *hold hands.*)

Executioner: Aaannd . . .

(*A* **Colonel** *of the Space Pandas appears.*)

Colonel: Wait!

George *(sighing):* What? *(Aside:)* Can you beat this? *(To* **Retainer***:)* Who is this guy?

Retainer: Who are you?

Colonel: "Fiat Tibi Quo Pax."

All: "Eee I Eee I Oh."

Colonel: Sire, I am Colonel Lazlo Drurik of the 58th Space Pandas, currently deployed on Asteroid five-eighteen of the Goolagong Euclidic Archipelago.

George: How are things up there?

Colonel: Sire, we have been overrun. We're overnumbered and outflanked. Our soldiers fall like flies. We were betrayed, our maps and plans were bartered to the enemy. They crept in while we slept and took the garrison. Only two escaped.

(One **Space Panda** *talks to another.)*

Panda 1: What did this guy say his name was?

Panda 2: Uh, Colonel Drurik.

Panda 1: I think I've heard of him, that sounds familiar.

(As the **Colonel** *talks, he surreptitiously slips the locks of the Concentration Chamber, and then draws the attention of the assemblage away from same.)*

George *(to* **Retainer***):* I seem to have heard this before . . .

Colonel: And I call for revenge, Lord, revenge on the dastardly cowards who crept in the night like worms . . .

Panda 1: Isn't that the Colonel's name in "Revenge of the Space Pandas"?

Panda 2: You know, you're right.

Panda 1: Maybe they modeled him after this guy.

Panda 2: Yeah.

(**Binky** *and* **Vivian** *sneak out of the booth and rendezvous with* **Bob**.)

Colonel: Revenge for the Honor of the Space Pandas and of Crestview. Those brave men and women will not have expired in vain. I call all citizens to arms . . .

George: I'm *sure* I've heard this . . .

Colonel: For the flag and the posterity of Crestview, of the Goolagong, of the Goose Nebula Herself, Sisters and Brothers, now, the time has come to . . .

George: *Wait* a second . . . *(Pause.)* We aren't at war with anyone. *(Pause.)* And furthermore, I've heard that speech somewhere before.

Executioner: Yeah.

George: Now, what is your name?

Colonel: Colonel Lazlo Drurik of the 58th Space Pandas.

George: Lazlo Drurik.

Executioner: Isn't that the Colonel's name in "Revenge of the Space . . ."

George: That's the speech from "The Revenge of the . . ."

Colonel: Run Vivian, run, Bob.

(*All eyes turn on* **Binky**, **Bob** *and* **Vivian**, *who make a mad dash for the two-speed clock, ensconced near the Throne of Topax.*)

Retainer: Stop them!

(Everyone tries, save **George**, *who continues conversing with* **Drurik**.*)*

George: Yeah. That's the speech from "Revenge of the Space Pandas."

Drurik: That is correct.

George: That is the speech from the *movie!!!* I *thought* so. *(Aside:)* Will somebody seize that sheep? *(To* **Colonel**:*)* So you aren't Lazlo Drurik. Is that what you're telling us?

Drurik: Sadly, yes.

George: Bad luck for you, then, turkey, 'cause you're in some real hot water here.

(The **Retainers** *catch the sheep.)*

Retainer: Hey, hey. We got him.

George: Took your own sweet time.

Retainer: We've recaptured the earthlings, your Lucidity.

George: Okay, okay. *(To* **earthlings**:*)* We're getting to you in a minute. Yeah. *(To crowd:)* Can you believe this? Here this tunafish just tritzes in, pretends to be a Colonel of the Great Space Pandas, gets us in a lather, huh, the whole time he's this dirty turncoat in league with the earthlings. *(Pause.)* What shall we do to him?

Retainer: Bad things.

George: You bet your life. *(To* **Drurik**:*)* I hope you got a taste for pumpkin, Boyo. *(***Crowd** *drools appreciatively.)* Who are you by the way?

(The **Colonel** *removes his mask. Astonished gasps.)*

Several: It's Edward *Farpis!!!*

George: Are you who you look like?

Farpis: Yes.

George: You're Edward Farpis?

Farpis: Yes.

George: Whatever *happened* to you?

Edward: I grew old.

George: You know, my parents took me to see you in "Beast of the Goolagong" when I was four years old. First movie I ever saw. *(Pause.)* Do you think that I might, have, you know, have an, I've got this cousin who just adores you and I wonder if you might, like, autograph my . . . *(To* **Retainer***:)* Gimme a piece of paper! *(To* **Farpis***:)* . . . thing to send to her. *(***Edward** *shrugs.)* Thank you, she'd, you know, really appreciate it.

(Paper and pen are brought by the **Retainer***.)*

Edward: What shall I say?

George: Just say . . .

Edward *(maneuvering):* You know, the light isn't really too good here . . . *(He steps back from throne.)*

George: Just say: "To my friend, George, a Great man, a Great leader . . . "

*(***Edward** *dashes to the clock and throws it to* **Binky***.)*

Binky: Oh, my gosh, does anybody have a bobbypin?

Bob: Viv?

*(***Vivian** *is holding off the hordes of attacking* **Space Pandas** *with karate.)*

Vivian: No. I've got a paper clip . . .

Binky: Well, let me have it.

Vivian (*reaching into her back pocket*): Here. It's on my science paper.

Binky: No. I really couldn't . . .

Vivian: Binky, for goodness sake . . . (*Thrusting paper and clip upon him.*)

Binky: Oh, alright. (*Takes paper clip.*)

George (*continuing*): " . . . a true friend of the Grey Goose Nebula . . ."

Binky (*under his breath*): This may just work . . .

Vivian: Oh, Binky . . .

Bob: I sure hope this thing works . . .

(**Binky** *continues to fumble with the clock.*)

George: "A constant source of inspiration, and a never-failing fount of humor and encouragement."

Vivian: You'd better hurry.

George (*going on*): " . . . I will never forget the afternoon that we spent in your throne room . . ."

Binky: I think I've got it. Yes, I've got it.

Edward: Goodbye, my friends!

Vivian: Goodbye, Mr. Farpis!

Bob: Goodbye, Ed, and thank you!

Vivian: I'm sorry that we doubted you.

Bob: Me, too . . .

George (*continuing*): " . . . and insights both on Politics and Art you shared with me . . ."

Edward: Goodnight, goodnight, goodnight.

(There is an explosion and **Bob**, **Binky** *and* **Vivian** *vanish.)*

George: ". . . and how . . ." What happened? *(Pause.)* Well, what happened?

Retainer: Sire, the earthsheep has escaped.

George *(to* **Executioner***):* Whack this man out. *(The* **Executioner** *comes and takes the* **Retainer** *over to the Concentration Booth.)* They got away? *(Pause.)* Well, did they get away? *(Pause.)*

Edward: They have escaped.

George *(pauses and then groans):* Nyahhheh!

Panda 1: What shall we do with this guy, Sire? *(Pause.)* Sire?

George: This *guy* is . . . You know who this guy is?

Panda 1: Edward Farpis.

George: Mr. Farpis, I saw you in "Penguins on Parade" at least six times.

Edward: You did?

George: You bet. You know that scene you play with Barbara Buffington?

Edward: The beach scene?

George: Yes. In that part where you go . . . How does the line go?

Edward *(as they talk, they walk off together):* "Grace I've been rich, and I've been poor. I've been twice around the Solar System, and they know my name on Luna and on Betelgeuse . . ."

George: That's it . . . *(They exit.)*

(The **Court Jester** *comes on.)*

Court Jester:

Oh, the Actor had come on (La La)
To help them get away. (La La)
And he'd brought along his Panda suit,
To help him save the day.
But when the Sheep and Earthlings . . .

*(***Topax** *returning, gestures the* **Jester** *into the Concentration Booth.)*

Jester *(under his breath):* Everyone's a critic . . .

George: A guy blows his one chance to get his letter sweater. You think someone might understand, huh? No. *(Sighs.)* But life goes on. *(Pause.)* Alright. Everybody take a break.

Retainer: FALL OUT FOR ANTHRACITE!

*(***Everybody** *falls out.)*

George: So, Ed—you don't mind if I call you Ed?

Edward: No. Not at all.

George: So, Ed, so tell me: What was Lola Laguna *really* like?

(The two walk off together.)

Scene Eight

Back in Waukegan, at the attic laboratory of **Binky Rudich**. **Mrs. Rudich** *is frozen in the same position in which we left her. Everybody unfreezes.*

Mrs. Rudich: If you think that I'm ever going to make you pizza when you want it when you can't come down to lunch once like a decent human being . . .

Binky: We've been up on Crestview, Mom.

Mrs. Rudich: Been where?

Vivian: On Crestview, Mrs. Rudich, the Pearl of the Goose Nebula.

Bob: That's right.

Mrs. Rudich: Well, that's no excuse, Leonard, Bob . . . when you know that lunch is ready, you should come downstairs. Especially when we've got company.

Vivian: I was up there, too.

Mrs. Rudich: Well, you're back now, and I think we'll go downstairs and . . . *(To Bob:)* I made casserole, Bob.

Bob: Mmmm!

Mrs. Rudich: Have some lunch and you all can go back to Crestwood when we're done.

Binky: Crest*view*, Mom.

Mrs. Rudich: Well, wherever it is. Alright? *(They nod.)* Good. *(She looks at two-speed clock.)* I mean, it's almost twelve-fifteen.

Binky: I think that clock is fast, Mom.

Mrs. Rudich: Yes, yes. Alright. *(Pause.)* Well, shall we go to lunch? *(Moment. General consent.)* Good. *(She starts for the door, followed by the stalwart three.)* Did you read in the papers about how they're going to have that travel pill soon, Leonard?

Binky: Bob was telling me.

Mrs. Rudich: I think it's wonderful the things they're coming up with.

Binky: Mmm. (**Mrs. Rudich** *exits. The three hang back. Pause.*) Well . . .

Vivian: Glad we're back, Bink?

Binky: I don't know, I guess I am. Bob?

Bob: Tell the truth, I'm kind of hungry.

Vivian: Yeah. I am, too.

Binky: *Shall* we?

Bob: Sure. (*The three start to leave.*)

Vivian: And maybe after lunch we'll see if we can get some other place.

Binky: We can only try, Viv.

(*The three stand around, then* **Binky** *and* **Vivian** *slowly and reluctantly go off toward the door.* **Bob** *starts singing, softly, to himself.*)

Bob: " . . . as we tool along through the Goolagong . . .

(**Binky** *and* **Vivian** *join in, and as the three sing, they get louder.*)

All: "We know you belong on your Big Fat Throne, so Hail to thee, George Topax,
Never 'gainst the Foe lax —
Fiat Tibi Quo Pax . . ."

Mrs. Rudich (*offstage*): *Lunchtime!!!*

(*They all stop singing, shrug. Hold.*)

Bob: Coming, Mrs. R.

(*They exit off to lunch.*)

L'envoi

Here's to you, Sweet Crestview —
As we bid you now Adieu.
Sweetheart of Space Factor Five,
Our hearts belong to you.
We hail your golden Kapoks
And your creamy Lunafish
To tritze along your Orange streets
Is yet our fondest wish.
Goodbye to you, Dear Crestview,
And to Topax, too, "So long."
As decrepit we grow
It's a comfort to know
We have been to the Goolagong.

L'ENVOI

From

The Revenge of the Space Pandas

Lyrics by David Mamet © 1976
music by Alaric Jans © 1977

Here's to you, sweet Crest-view As we bid you now A- . dieu Sweet-heart of Space Sec-tor Five, Our hearts be-long to you. We hail your gol-den Ka-poks and your cream-y Lu-na-Fish To tritze a-long your

THE GOOLAGONG ANTHEM

Lyrics by David Mamet © 1976
Music by Alaric Jans © 1977